MW00462915

Abraham
and Straus

You might think of Michael Lisicky's obsession with department stores as an orchestral tone poem for a single oboe: by turns plaintive and raucous, eloquent and funny, with unpredictable little swerves.
—Baltimore Sun

In a book jammed full of fun facts, Lisicky clearly relays his love for department stores.
—Newark Star-Ledger

Lisicky's book thoroughly details [the department store] *and arouses a rush of nostalgia.*
—New Jersey Monthly

Retail fans can now take a stroll down memory lane with Lisicky, a department store historian.
—Boston Globe

Lisicky is probably the only department store historian I know. He's an oboist with the Baltimore Symphony but his true passion is those great brick-and-mortar stores that were so much a part of our lives.
—Tampa Tribune

Like many people, Lisicky figured department stores—these massive temples of commerce that sold everything from sewing supplies to fancy furs—would endure. A baby boomer born in 1964, the author loved how each American city had its own department store, such as Hudson's in Detroit and Marshall Field's in Chicago. [But now] *while he earns his living as a professional musician, Mr. Lisicky's other love is writing books about department stores that have disappeared.*
—Pittsburgh Post-Gazette

Like veterans of a noble cause—a battle or an expedition—former employees of Woodward & Lothrop came forward to share their memories after the recent column on Lisicky's book. Customers did, too.
—Washington Post

If you're interested in department store history, buy his books.
—Philadelphia Inquirer

MICHAEL J. LISICKY

Abraham and Straus

It's Worth a Trip from Anywhere

THE
History
PRESS

Published by The History Press
Charleston, SC
www.historypress.net

Copyright © 2017 by Michael J. Lisicky
All rights reserved

Images courtesy of author unless otherwise noted.

First published 2017

Manufactured in the United States

ISBN 9781625858870

Library of Congress Control Number: 2017948450

Notice: The information in this book is true and complete to the best of our knowledge. It is offered without guarantee on the part of the author or The History Press. The author and The History Press disclaim all liability in connection with the use of this book.

All rights reserved. No part of this book may be reproduced or transmitted in any form whatsoever without prior written permission from the publisher except in the case of brief quotations embodied in critical articles and reviews.

For Tillie,

my four-legged Funny Face.

Contents

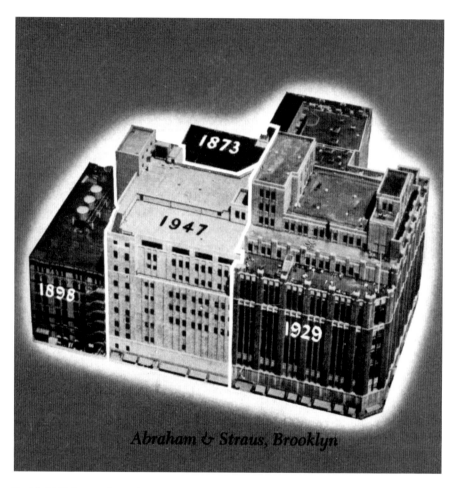

In this 1948 image, the various sections of the Fulton Street store are divided by their dates of construction. This image compilation focuses on the store's Livingston Street frontage.

Abraham & Straus was an enormous factor growing up on the shopping end of things in Brooklyn. My mom and I, along with my younger sisters, pretty much grew up in poverty and lived in public housing. Abraham & Straus was a store that we'd visit on Fulton Street, but my mom would basically take us to Mays. It was probably among the least expensive retailers at that time. We went to Abraham & Straus in amazement and wonder, but I don't believe my mother ever bought anything from there. Certainly by the time I became older I went to Abraham & Straus all the time. It was our Bloomingdale's, our Neiman Marcus, our Nordstrom's all wrapped up into one. That's the best way to put it. It was a fabulous store.

—Marty Markowitz, former Brooklyn Borough president and New York State senator, March 20, 2017

A&S, Brooklyn's best department store in my growing-up years. There, one could shop to satisfy both household and personal needs. Reasonable prices, though for Depression babies like me, Ohrbach's and Klein's across the bridge offered better bargains. A&S was downtown from my Kings Highway neighborhood, at or near Fulton Street, not far from Borough Hall. Years later, in my college years, I worked as a summer salesperson at the spacious A&S in Hempstead.

—the Honorable Ruth Bader Ginsburg, associate justice, Supreme Court of the United States, March 13, 2017

Acknowledgements

This book could not have been made possible without the generous help from numerous individuals and archival organizations. Sincere thanks go to the Brooklyn Historical Society, along with staff members Tess Colwell and John Zarrillo, for keeping history alive at their institution and allowing me to research their A&S collection. Additional appreciation goes to the Brooklyn Public Library and its Brooklyn Collection room. The library's website affords free access to the *Brooklyn Daily Eagle* archives to all. Newspapers played an important role in documenting history and continue to provide this necessary benefit. The *Daily Eagle*'s archives, from 1841 until its final January 28, 1955 edition, are available at our fingertips twenty-four hours a day, without cost. The department store's earliest history was best uncovered thanks to this amazing resource. Additional insight into A&S was provided by Abraham family member Walter "Trip" Rothschild III and Diane Straus through the assistance of Joan Adler, executive director of the Straus Historical Society.

Numerous executives and associates answered my calls and provided personal details and stories about this iconic Brooklyn institution. Chaim Edelstein, Curtis Champlin, Mel Wilmore, Bill Laupus, Douglas Schuler, Mary Jane Solino, Valerie Capobianco and Lasker Meyer helped bring A&S's corporate past to life. Incredible gratitude goes to Scott Snyder, who generously allowed me to reprint some rare branch store images and shared his personal passion and continued dedication to A&S's. Without Mr. Snyder's social media presence on A&S, I would not have been afforded an important photographic contribution from Frank Nieves Jr. Thanks to years of research, all photos in this book come from my personal collection unless otherwise noted.

Over the years, I have been thrilled and honored to receive personal memories from many celebrities and dignitaries who have shared their stories about these beloved stores. Three prominent individuals helped make this A&S book special and belong to Brooklynites. Those individuals are former borough president and former state senator Marty Markowitz, City Councilman of Brooklyn's Forty-Sixth District Alan N. Maisel and the Honorable Ruth Bader Ginsburg, associate justice, Supreme Court of the United States, through the assistance of U.S. Supreme Court public information officer Kathleen L. Arberg.

Always at my side providing support and information are Jan Whitaker and David Sullivan, along with Bruce Kopytek at the Department Store Museum website. Appreciation goes to The History Press and Arcadia Publishing for allowing me to complete this ten-book series on America's department stores. But without my wife, Sandy, you wouldn't be able to understand or read a thing. Sandy has been standing by me with every book, asking hundreds of questions that needed clarification and rewording thousands of prepositional phrases since 2009.

Introduction

Sometimes I forget that A&S is still open, at least in some form. There are so few downtown department stores left in this country. These remaining stores seem to be either important icons or faded relics. Every year, it seems as though another one bites the dust and its hometown is devastated, even though its residents had largely abandoned it as part of their shopping and social scene years ago.

It's easy to think of New York as just Manhattan, especially from an outsider's perspective. The other boroughs might appear to be a collection of neighborhoods, strong and weak, that just feed off Manhattan. But that is not the case, and it certainly is not the case with Brooklyn. Brooklyn has a tremendous history and is a major city within itself. Its working-class roots have either maintained their melting pot image or have transitioned into new wealth. And through it all, it's proud of its identity. Through it all, the building that housed America's third-largest department store complex is still open for business and plays a pivotal role in downtown Brooklyn's revival.

Abraham & Straus grew up with Brooklyn, and Brooklyn grew up with Abraham & Straus. Many Brooklynites were unable to afford making regular shopping excursions to A&S, but they still relied on the store for holiday traditions and community sponsorships. Abraham & Straus was happy to oblige, and that was part of its legacy.

As "the Store Grew in Brooklyn," Abraham & Straus expanded beyond Brooklyn and into other close and distant communities. Its 1952 Hempstead store was a marvel and is often revered by department store enthusiasts.

It served Long Island residents who grew tired of getting on a train or driving long distances. After it added two additional floors to its original two-story structure, A&S Hempstead became the country's largest suburban department store. Although there were other A&S branches, few could match the size and strength of Hempstead. That's how it also seemed on Fulton Street. But after four decades of service, A&S Hempstead turned from a relevant behemoth to a white elephant. Some saw the former Fulton Street flagship in that very same light. However, in the end, that old Brooklyn store, unlike so many other amazing downtown department stores, is still open for business—at least in some form.

I am admittedly an outsider, not to the department store world but to New York City and, more specifically, Brooklyn. I grew up near Philadelphia, where John Wanamaker, Strawbridge & Clothier, Gimbels and, later on, Bamberger's ruled the roost. When Abraham & Straus entered the Philadelphia market in 1981, I was anxious to pay it a visit. As I walked through the store, I knew that there was a problem: A&S was not Philadelphia. The store was loaded with glitz and chrome, and Philadelphia is not a glitz-and-chrome market. Philadelphia was competitive and crowded and largely consisted of traditionally frayed or realistically conservative retailers. Abraham & Straus was neither. A&S didn't last long in Philadelphia, but as the years marched on, neither did much of its competition.

As a historian, I look back in awe at Abraham & Straus. The company, along with Filene's, gave birth to the legendary Federated Department Stores company right on the family's yacht. Federated eventually grew into America's premier department store holding company. (The word *premier* is arguable.) And A&S's Fulton Street flagship grew into America's third-largest department store. That, too, is arguable. (I never got on my hands and knees with a ruler and measured every floor. I would need to do the same at Chicago's Marshall Field building. I don't have that option at Detroit's J.L. Hudson, the country's undisputed second-largest store, as that icon was closed in 1983 and imploded in 1998.)

Within these pages, the story of Abraham & Straus is largely told. At times, it goes hand and hand with the story of Brooklyn. Its history deserves to be in print. As of 2017, the former downtown A&S continues to welcome area residents and workers. The building is experiencing a massive redevelopment. It is no longer the country's third-, or fourth-, largest department store. Its floor size has dropped from 1.6 million square feet to just over 270,000. It may not be the same store that Brooklyn, and other borough residents, remembers, but its legacy is well worth documenting and celebrating.

CHAPTER 1

Opportunity Days

Since its founding, Abraham & Straus had, at its hand, men of vision, character,
and leadership. It was not solely occupied with selling goods, and making a
profit. It was interested in having a store that played a very important part of the
community, which is Brooklyn.
—Walter Rothschild Sr., grandson of company founder Abraham Abraham,
December 1, 1953

Back in the 1860s, Brooklyn, with a population of approximately 300,000 residents, was America's third-largest city. In the early half of the nineteenth century, its farmlands supplied wheat, corn and potatoes to neighboring communities. Brooklyn was home to everything from horse stables to skating ponds, as well as some of the country's finest examples of Dutch architecture. "Brooklyn was just a placid, country town [in the 1860s]," stated an Abraham & Straus brochure from 1945. "Brooklyn belles wore billowing crinolines and coaches clattered over the cobblestone streets."[1]

Brooklyn was home to a variety of industries, and its busy waterfront was lined with warehouses. Ships delivered sugar, molasses, honey and cotton to its surrounding area. During the nineteenth century, Brooklyn grew into a diverse community and was home to many Irish, German and English residents. As its population grew, Brooklynites demanded greater services and amenities. In 1865, two enterprising young men opened a small dry goods establishment that developed over time into one of the country's leading and

Left: The original Wechsler & Abraham dry goods business at its 285 Fulton Street storefront.

Right: In February 1865, Abraham Abraham established the original business at age twenty-two. Members of the Abraham family worked in the store's management until 1969.

largest department stores. For three decades, Wechsler & Abraham was one of Brooklyn's leading retail houses.

Joseph Wechsler was born in Poppenhausen, Bavaria, and immigrated to New York in 1856, along with his mother and brothers Abraham, Samuel and Herman. For the next three years, Wechsler worked as a "humble peddler" and pushed carts throughout Brooklyn that contained dry goods and notions.[2] In 1859, Joseph, along with his brothers, opened a storefront at 137 Myrtle Avenue, between Gold and Duffield Streets. The Wechsler Bros. store offered "Dry Goods for the Million," and "customers, housekeepers, and parties coming from the country were respectfully invited" to view "the largest assortment of goods in the city, at retail for wholesale prices." Described as a person who was "quiet in his ways," Joseph Wechsler was a shrewd businessman.[3] He convinced his brothers to stock the business with Irish, French and German goods that catered to the area's immigrant population. The popular Wechsler Bros. establishment drew the attention of New York merchant Judah Abraham. After he developed a close business relationship with Joseph Wechsler, Judah invested in the Wechsler firm.

Abraham Abraham, the son of Judah Abraham and Susan Sussman, was born in his parents' New York Murray Street home on March 9, 1843. "[Abraham] must have had a lazy mother or else he would have had a different name," his grandson Walter Rothschild Sr. quipped in 1953. "Or else she liked alliteration." Throughout his early childhood, Abraham was plagued with health problems, and his parents kept him from attending school. At age fourteen, he became a clerk at Newark's Hart & Dettlebach dry goods firm and worked alongside young Simon Bloomingdale and Benjamin Altman. Within two years, Abraham was named head of the shawl department and earned a salary of $8 per week.

When the Civil War commenced, Abraham traveled to Chicago, intending to enlist in the Union army. Thwarted by his parents, Abraham returned to New York and worked in a variety of area stores. Abraham ultimately settled on Brooklyn's Wechsler Bros. The Wechslers provided him with room and board in addition to his salary. The ambitious Abraham ultimately wanted to open his own dry goods store. Lacking the financial capital necessary, he convinced Joseph Wechsler to partner in a new business. With $8,000 from Joseph Wechsler and $4,000 from Abraham Abraham, the Wechsler & Abraham dry goods business was born.[4]

Abraham persuaded Wechsler to locate their new business on Fulton Street, Brooklyn's most fashionable thoroughfare. Fulton Street was a heavily traveled street that led to the Fulton Ferry, Brooklyn's connection to Manhattan. On Fulton Street, "crowds of ladies and children, misses and pet poodles, promenade[d] the sidewalk even down to the river."[5] On February 14, 1865, Wechsler & Abraham celebrated its grand opening at 285 Fulton Street. Promoted as a "Dry Goods, Shawl, and Cloak Emporium," Wechsler & Abraham was stocked with shawls, capes, ribbons, millinery, velvets and woolens. Merely twenty-five feet wide and ninety feet long, Wechsler & Abraham employed only three workers. Its grand opening notice in the *Brooklyn Daily Eagle* proclaimed its "reasonable prices with polite and attentive clerks."[6]

"Abraham & Straus [Wechsler & Abraham] started at a rather unfortunate time," recalled Abraham Abraham's grandson Walter Rothschild Sr. Heavy rain drenched Brooklyn on the store's opening day. "[Abraham] spent most of the day with his nose glued against the door, looking out in the mess for perspective customers," remembered Rothschild in 1953. "To make matters worse, his banker was there and [Abraham] was practically sure [his banker] was going to call the loan on him." The outbreak of the Civil War also threatened the business's success. The two partners had purchased

GREAT DECLINE IN DRY GOODS,
WECHSLER & ABRAHAM,
285 FULTON ST.,
Are now offering their immense stock of
DRY GOODS
at greatly reduced prices. For instance:
SPRING POPLINS, (splendid quality), 25, 30, 37 and 5
cts per yard
DELAINES, (best make.) 25 cts.
Also Housekeeping Goods, comprising Linen Sheetings,
2 yards wide, 87 cts per yard. Linen Sheetings, 2½ yards
wide, $1 37 and $1 50 per yard, Crumb Cloth, all linen. 3
yards wide $2 25. Also, Table Damask, Napkins, Diapers,
Towelings, Table Clothe, Bleached and Unbleached Cot-
tons, at proportionately low prices.
Housekeepers desirous of laying in their supplies will
find it to their interest to inspect our stock before purchas-
ing elsewhere.
WECHSLER & ABRAHAM,
m3 t*   285 Fulton street.

In 1866, the *Brooklyn Daily Eagle* published a Wechsler & Abraham advertisement that stressed the store's excess of stock.

their stock during the peak of inflation. "The war sent prices sky high," said Rothschild. "The war stopped, the prices tumbled and there we were with a big stock."[7]

Exactly two months after the store's opening day, President Abraham Lincoln was assassinated. As the community mourned, many Brooklyn business owners placed memorial displays in their street windows. Featuring a bust of the fallen president, Wechsler & Abraham's store window was "wildly commented on." "I had seen [a bust of Lincoln] in a barber shop and when the tragedy occurred I secured it at once," said Abraham in 1908. "The pedestal [in the display window] was draped in black and white silk and on it hung a quotation from 'Hamlet.'"[8] As Lincoln's death led to an era of economic instability, Wechsler & Abraham persevered and kept all bills current.

When it initially opened for business, Wechsler & Abraham leased the entire four-story building but sublet the upper floors to renters. "I remember there was a photographer just above [our original] store and over him a dentist; who was subsequently shot while passing through City Park down near the Navy Yard, and his murder created quite a stir," said Abraham.[9] Wechsler & Abraham embarked on the first of a series of expansions that transformed the small dry goods store into one of Brooklyn's largest and most respected businesses.

In October 1867, Wechsler & Abraham stopped leasing out the upper floors and began utilizing the entire four-story building. The *Brooklyn Daily Eagle* reported, "One of the most enterprising and most popular dry goods stores in the City of Churches, enlarged their handsome establishment and doubled its size." In October 1873, the store completed a three-story addition, doubling in size again. A Washington Street entrance was created, and the structure's addition included a basement. Wechsler & Abraham became a formidable option for shoppers who traditionally traveled to Manhattan. "With each recurring season, the business establishments of Brooklyn enter into closer rivalry in extent and magnitude with those of the Metropolis across the East River," stated an 1873 *Brooklyn Daily Eagle* report.

In August 1876, Wechsler & Abraham acquired the neighboring Willoughby mansion on Washington Street. The Willoughby mansion was replaced by a new structure that allowed for the addition of home furnishings and increased the store's square footage to thirty thousand square feet. The *Brooklyn Daily Eagle* reported, "Wechsler & Abraham first formed in Brooklyn twelve years ago, and since that time it has steadily grown in prosperity and popularity until to-day it has no rivals."

In 1867, a new rapid transit elevated train line was proposed along Fulton Street. The planned transit line was designed to facilitate travel along Fulton Street, from Bedford-Stuyvesant down to the Fulton Ferry. The elevated train received support from Brooklyn's business community, but its planning and development were plagued by constant cries of corruption. Joseph Wechsler and Abraham Abraham differed on their opinions of the new train. In an 1879 *Brooklyn Daily Eagle* opinion column, Joseph Wechsler stated that the elevated rapid transit line "will do us [Wechsler & Abraham] a great deal of harm. I think it will stop shopping on this thoroughfare very considerably. Besides that, I think if we get rapid transit to the ferry, it will carry the trade to New York." In contrast, Abraham Abraham saw the transit line as a mode of transportation in Brooklyn that facilitated shopping within the city limits. For years, Abraham "labored" for the Fulton Street transit line project.[10]

In the 1820s, community leaders discussed the creation of a bridge between New York and Brooklyn. Although there was a desire to link the two cities, some feared that a new bridge could drain population and commerce from Brooklyn. Over the years, ferry service between New York and Brooklyn grew unreliable, and a new bridge became a necessity. Construction of the iconic Brooklyn Bridge began in 1869. As construction costs increased, the original $5 million price tag swelled to $15 million. Abraham Abraham publicly championed the bridge. Abraham "had the foresight to know that the bridge would stimulate the growth of both the Brooklyn and Manhattan communities." He called the Brooklyn Bridge, with its mighty towers, massive cables and graceful arch, "the eighth wonder of the world." In honor of the bridge's dedication on May 24, 1883, Wechsler & Abraham decorated a show window with a "symbolic group" of eight electrical lights.

A spring/summer 1886 Wechsler & Abraham catalogue states that the Brooklyn store is "the Mecca of Long Island." The three bottom sketches from left to right depict the Ladies' Parlor, the Gallatin Place entrance and the Livingston Street entrance.

In 1883, Brooklyn was not wired for power, but the store's personal generator powered the electrical lights.

Of the two partners, Abraham was the more visible figurehead and visionary, while Wechsler worked behind the scenes and dealt with the store's buying and personnel matters. The new Brooklyn Bridge provided an opportunity for both men to think big and explore continued growth. Wechsler & Abraham took a large risk and relocated its store. Its new building, located near the Brooklyn Bridge entryway, defined a retail core for Brooklyn.

CHAPTER 2

Wheeler's Folly

At first the undertaking appeared too rash, too bold, too big, by far too anticipatory for Brooklyn. But Brooklyn has been underrated in the past.
—Brooklyn Daily Eagle, *July 27, 1892*

In December 1873, Brooklyn real estate investor Andrew S. Wheeler completed a five-story building at 424 Fulton Street between Gallatin Place and Hoyt Street. The structure was designed to accommodate luxurious retail shops, prime office space and other commercial needs. It also housed a ballroom named Gallatin Hall. Located many blocks from Brooklyn's established commercial heart, the Wheeler Building was ridiculed and experienced poor occupancy rates. After ten years, it "degenerated into tenancy by small cheap shops," including an auction house and sideshow attractions such as General Tom Thumb and his "Charming Little Wife."[11] Brooklyn's residents called the building "Wheeler's Folly," and its owner was eager to sell his property.

Fulton Street beyond Flatbush Avenue resembled "a western mining town." According to company history, Abraham Abraham went for a half-mile walk and came upon the five-story Wheeler Building. The large structure was clearly underutilized and in need of repair. Abraham stated, "Like a flash, it came to me that when the Brooklyn Bridge opened, that part of Fulton Street could be made the center of Brooklyn."[12] Abraham "brought his partner Wechsler to his way of thinking," and the two men quietly entered negotiations for the Wheeler Building.[13]

On February 1, 1883, Wechsler & Abraham surprised the Brooklyn community and officially purchased the Wheeler Building. Critics openly chastised the two merchants and stated they were "cutting their own throats." It was "doing a suicidal thing to leave the excellent business it enjoyed a half a dozen blocks lower down the street and attempt, by one great wrench, to change the current of feminine shoppers, on which it as well as the other large houses of the same kind depended."[14]

The criticism did not deter their move, and the two men reconfigured their new building. Its 101-foot Fulton Street frontage and 187-foot depth provided five times the size of the lower Fulton Street location. The interior of the former Wheeler Building was largely demolished and rebuilt. The centerpiece of the renovation was a five-story central rotunda. A highly ornamental glass dome illuminated the building. Gold-colored railings, Corinthian pillars, silver-leafed columns and a large clock on a bronze stand helped fill the impressive space. A three-story ornamental arch graced the Fulton Street exterior. The new home of Wechsler & Abraham, with its signature mansard roof, transformed a large, irrelevant structure into one of Brooklyn's most conspicuous buildings.

Wechsler & Abraham opened its "magnificent new dry goods store" on Monday, February 16, 1885. It was promoted as "the largest and best equipped store in America." The firm stated that "the big store will be a spectacle and a show for a time, and then the ladies of the city will wonder how they ever managed to get along without this beautiful new establishment."[15] With more than forty separate departments, Wechsler & Abraham offered laces, jewelry, notions, "made to order" shoes, gentlemen's furnishings, housekeeping goods, carpets, china, an entire floor devoted to furniture, a Ladies' Parlor and an elegant Dark Room that displayed rich evening fabrics and silks by gaslight. The store proclaimed that the Dark Room and the Ladies' Parlor would "not be surpassed by the chief houses of New York."[16]

The new Wechsler & Abraham symbolized a coming of age for Brooklyn. Although it was home to more than 700,000 residents, Brooklyn had lived in the shadow of New York, just across the harbor. In 1908, Abraham Abraham reflected on the firm's 1885 expansion and said, "It took the Bridge to create a sense of Brooklyn city identity. The new store was a symbol, clear evidence of city power and pride. Brooklyn women were delighted in being able to buy so successfully at home, and began to apologize if they crossed to Manhattan."[17]

Located away from Brooklyn's traditional commercial center, Wechsler & Abraham attracted approximately forty thousand customers every day.

Annual sales reached $2.5 million. In April 1886, an addition included a new entrance along Livingston Street. "They will have extended all their departments and added so many new ones that it will be pretty hard to name an article which cannot be purchased there," reported the *Brooklyn Daily Eagle*. A large candy counter "where ladies can buy caramels and the other sweet things with which they solace themselves and spoil their teeth" complemented a modern food department that sold produce, meat and fish.[18] The business added a new postal order service and charge account program. As Wechsler & Abraham grew in popularity, established businesses moved to the store's vicinity, and Brooklyn's new business district took shape.

Abraham Abraham and Joseph Wechsler's successful new store attracted attention within the burgeoning international department store industry. It was compared to Wanamaker's in Philadelphia, A.T. Stewart in New York, Whiteley's in London and the Bon Marché in Paris. Smaller, more specialized businesses located throughout Brooklyn were threatened by Wechsler & Abraham. The five-story building could offer a greater assortment of goods with lower prices than most businesses.

On October 28, 1887, a package arrived at Joseph Wechsler's home. When his wife opened the package in her husband's absence, an explosion by "an infernal machine" severely injured Mrs. Wechsler. Some reports stated that her wounds "would disfigure her for life."[19] Wechsler's ten-year-old grandson, Philip, was injured as pieces of wood and metal exploded from the package. The incident became the subject of a massive police hunt. Wechsler was distraught and confused by the attack, believing it to be the work of a disgruntled employee. The Wechsler & Abraham store offered a $925 reward for the apprehension of the person or persons involved in the attempt on Joseph Wechsler's life.

The case was never solved, but the package contained an anonymous note written by a "tinsmith." The note stated that Wechsler & Abraham was responsible for putting the man out of business. Months prior to the incident, the *Brooklyn Daily Eagle* received a letter that "infernal machines" were placed throughout the large store: "I thought I would give you time to warn your friends to keep away from [Wechsler & Abraham] as their lives would be endangered." The note was traced back to a small fancy goods store, and the threat was looked on as "a scheme on the part of someone to injure [Wechsler & Abraham's] holiday trade."[20]

By 1889, Wechsler & Abraham, with 200,000 square feet of space, had become the largest retail business in the state of New York.[21] Two passenger elevators, installed in 1889, were met with fear and skepticism by some

In 1885, Wechsler & Abraham moved to 422 Fulton Street and advertised itself as "the Largest Dry Goods House in the State."

customers. "At first, [customers] approached [the elevators] as if they were going to take a ride in a 'Chute the Chutes' at an amusement park," recalled manager George Sullivan in 1935.[22] On April 30, 1889, Wechsler & Abraham celebrated the 100th anniversary of George Washington's inauguration. More than 2,800 yards of bunting decorated the building, and a twenty-four-foot-tall bronze bust of Washington was placed on a bronze pedestal on the first floor. In September 1889, Wechsler & Abraham made history and installed an electric arc of lights that consisted of sixty two-hundred-candlepower bulbs. The revolutionary light display was powered by the store's own power plant, regarded at the time as the largest private electric plant in the world.[23]

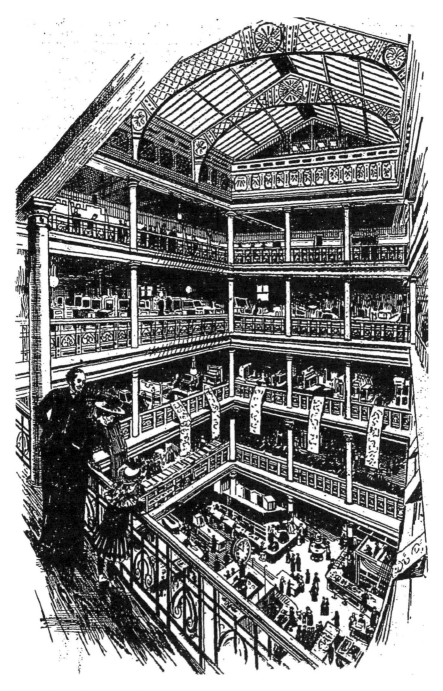

The interior of Wechsler & Abraham's new store included an impressive five-story rotunda surmounted by an ornamental glass dome.

ABRAHAM AND
STRAUS·
SUCCESSORS TO
WECHSLER & ABRAHAM

The business heretofore conducted under the firm name of WECHSLER & ABRAHAM, owing to the retiring of Mr. Joseph Wechsler, will be continued by the undersigned under the style of ABRAHAM & STRAUS.

ABRAHAM ABRAHAM,
ISIDOR STRAUS,
NATHAN STRAUS,
SIMON F. ROTHSCHILD.

We rarely speak of our ourselves, for "On their own merits modest men are dumb." The public learn in time to discriminate between the real and the unreal, and the twenty-eight years we have been in business has given the people ample time to become familiar with our virtues and our failings. That our methods in the past met with the approval of our patrons is proven by our enormous and constantly growing business—by far the largest in Brooklyn.

The policy that has proved so successful in the past will be rigidly adhered to in the future. We will continue to serve the public honestly with the best, at the lowest possible prices. The supremacy we have attained we will endeavor to retain. We will try to elevate our business to a still greater eminence, but never by intentional injury to competitors.

Our establishment is the largest in Brooklyn, none more beautiful or so large in New York. We are the recognized exponents of modern merchandising in this city, and we will do our best to maintain the distinction. The reorganized firm, strengthened by the addition of younger men, yet thoroughly equipped with business experience, is apt to do no less hereafter.

Deeply grateful to our friends and patrons for their many courtesies and kind wishes, we will demonstrate in the future, by our efforts, to deserve a continued recognition of their esteem and favor.

For Monday, believe us, we have made preparations to celebrate the change of the personnel of the firm in a way not soon to be forgotten—Each of the three score and seven departments will bristle with spring's fresh goods, fashions and enterprise leaders.

Manage somehow to "do" the store Monday.

ABRAHAM AND
STRAUS·
SUCCESSORS TO
WECHSLER & ABRAHAM

On April 1, 1893, the business was officially renamed Abraham & Straus. Its opening announcement asked shoppers to "manage somehow to 'do' the store" on its first day of operation. In 1893, Abraham & Straus featured separate departments of merchandise.

In the fall of 1892, rumors surfaced that the partnership between Joseph Wechsler and Abraham Abraham had grown fragile. Word spread that the two men had not spoken to each other for months due to an unspecified business disagreement. On December 15, 1892, the store stunned Brooklyn and announced that the partnership between Joseph Wechsler and Abraham Abraham would be dissolved. The dissolution was effective February 1, 1893, and the store noted that "the personal feelings of the members of the firm are amicable, therefore, the final adjustment of their respective interests will be a mere routine affair."[24] Questioned by the *Brooklyn Daily Eagle*, Joseph Wechsler gave assurance that "everything is perfectly lovely" between the two partners.

A letter to the *Brooklyn Daily Eagle* from a "company insider" called Abraham the better businessman of the two and noted that Abraham had grown tired of making up for Wechsler's shortcomings. The letter angered the Wechsler family and drew a quick response. "Mr. Abraham has been successful, but again his success, his fame, and his fortune is linked with the name of a Wechsler," stated an anonymous Wechsler family member.[25] In a December 24 editorial in the *Brooklyn Daily Eagle*, the newspaper urged the two men to reconsider their business separation.

A Christmas Eve message pleaded for reconciliation: "The inside energy of Mr. Wechsler and the skillful, pervasive and always outlooking quality of Mr. Abraham's talents have made the firm successful in its caretaking, and steady and expansive in its progress in all these eight and thirty years." The newspaper earnestly advised Wechsler & Abraham to "recall their notice of dissolution, quash whatever real or fancied division has grown up between them, agree not to canvass the causes, but never to refer to them at all, and preserve their active relations as if nothing had happened. We know the great home public of Brooklyn desires they should do so."[26] The newspaper plea did not persuade the two men to change their minds. Joseph Wechsler officially retired from the business on February 1, 1893, and received a $2.8 million payment from Abraham. Abraham Abraham found new partners, and the store continued on its explosive path of growth.

CHAPTER 3

The World's Largest Stores

While Isidor [Straus] *pretty much ran Macy's, Nathan had too much energy to be contained in an office.*
—*Joan Adler, executive director, Straus Historical Society*

During the fall of 1892, rumors abounded that Abraham Abraham had formed a partnership with Isidor and Nathan Straus. The Straus brothers were not strangers to the retail trade or Wechsler & Abraham. Both men owned and managed New York's venerable R.H. Macy & Company. In 1888, Isidor and Nathan Straus established a china and glass department at Wechsler & Abraham. On February 1, 1893, Wechsler & Abraham announced that Isidor and Nathan Straus had acquired Joseph Wechsler's stake in the store. The new business arrangement designated Abraham Abraham as the company's executive head and named son-in-law Simon F. Rothschild as a partner. Although they were partners, the Straus brothers served only in an advisory capacity to store management.

On April 1, 1893, Wechsler & Abraham was formally renamed Abraham & Straus. Although the *Brooklyn Daily Eagle* bemoaned the passing of the old name, it cited the changeover to Abraham & Straus as a symbol of the "progress of Brooklyn enterprise, industry, and thrift." The *Eagle* praised Abraham for "inaugurating the innovation of a department house in Brooklyn" and the Strauses for bringing "vast resources and output of European manufactories" to the Brooklyn store.[27] A company announcement noted that the Abraham & Straus store was "strengthened by the addition of

Left: Brothers Nathan, Oscar and Isidor Straus gather for a family portrait sometime at the turn of the century. Nathan and Isidor concentrated their managerial efforts on their R.H. Macy & Company business but became investment partners in Abraham & Straus in 1893. Isidor and his wife, Ida, succumbed in the RMS *Titanic* disaster in April 1912. *Courtesy of the Straus Historical Society*.

Below: An 1894 postcard shows Brooklyn's massive Abraham & Straus complex, along with the Fulton Street Elevated Line.

the young men [who were] thoroughly equipped with business experience." The "reorganized" Abraham & Straus was the New York Metropolitan Area's largest establishment.

In 1853, Isidor and Nathan Straus's father, Lazarus Straus, immigrated to America from Bavaria. He initially settled in Talbotton, Georgia, but relocated to New York City in 1865. Lazarus, along with his oldest son, Isidor, founded L. Straus & Son, a wholesale crockery house. Lazarus's sons, Nathan and Oscar, later joined the crockery firm. "As the oldest child of Lazarus and Sara Straus, Isidor took on the role as mentor to his siblings and it seems they all turned to him for guidance and direction," said Straus family historian Joan Adler.

By the 1880s, L. Straus & Sons had become the country's leading importer of pottery and china. On December 4, 1858, Rowland Hussey Macy opened a small dry goods store on New York's Fourteenth Street. Macy was regarded as a "prudent, energetic, and painstaking merchant."[28] As his business grew, he expanded into several adjoining buildings. In September 1874, L. Straus & Sons opened a large crockery department at R.H. Macy Company. After Macy passed away from kidney disease in 1877, Isidor and Nathan Straus acquired a large interest in the R.H. Macy store. In January 1888, the Straus brothers bought out a third partner, J.B. Webster, and became sole owners of the R.H. Macy & Company department store. "Isidor pretty much ran Macy's," stated Adler. "Nathan had too much energy to be contained in an office."

Although he advised Isidor on facets of the business and took frequent European buying trips, Nathan Straus was interested in philanthropy, even at an early age. "Nathan cared about people and did work hard for the family business," said Adler. "But as Isidor was always driven, thinking, and working [in business], Nathan seemed to have been a whirling dervish who spun himself out from time to time with his many activities." Affordable safe milk for infant nutrition was one of his most passionate causes. Nathan established special milk stations throughout the city that provided pasteurized milk from his own milk sterilizing plant. The Straus family's success allowed Nathan to combine his business skill and philanthropic goals. After he joined with the Straus brothers, Abraham Abraham advertised his business as a "department store," a recently coined term. These new department stores typically described massive emporiums that featured large selections of unique merchandise, along with guaranteed fair pricing and customer satisfaction.

When he sold his stake in Wechsler & Abraham, Joseph Wechsler signed an agreement that forbade him from operating a similar business for another five years. The agreement also restricted any other business from using his name. The day after the sale was finalized, Joseph Wechsler gave his sons, Louis and Aaron, $300,000 for investment in their own department store. The arrangement angered Abraham. A Wechsler family member insisted that "Mr. Joseph Wechsler will not have anything to do with the store but his patrons will know that he will see to it that his sons' store is what it should be. I expect the new store will get a good deal of the trade which formerly dealt with [Wechsler & Abraham]."[29]

Joseph Wechsler was Abraham's original partner in the department store. The partnership between the two businessmen deteriorated over time, and Wechsler left the firm in 1893.

A seven-story building at Fulton Street and Bedford Avenue was selected as the new store's location. Major Peter H. McNulty, a former manager at Wechsler & Abraham and future New York senator, became a partner in the new firm. On September 18, 1893, the new department store, Wechsler & McNulty, opened for business. The celebration featured a display of 360 incandescent lamps that spelled out "Grand Opening, Wechsler & McNulty." Additional lighting displays mounted on the building's exterior featured a spinning wheel, a moving time clock, a juggler and a dragon. The electrical display was designed and presented by the Edison Decorative and Miniature Lamp Department Company.

By 1895, Major McNulty was focused on real estate and political interests and left the store in June. The company changed its name to Joseph Wechsler's Sons after McNulty's departure. Much to the dismay of Abraham Abraham, Joseph Wechsler was a visible presence in his sons' store. "Scarcely a day passed that he was not around the store, taking the same interest in the business as in the days of active partnership."[30] Joseph Wechsler passed away on October 21, 1896, and the family learned that a provision in Joseph's will prevented his sons from operating the store without their father's managerial approval. The Joseph Wechsler's Sons department store closed abruptly on November 16, 1896.

Abraham & Straus thrived under its new business partnership, and the store continually expanded. A new carriage entrance was erected in 1896 along Livingston Street. Every expansion ensured that Abraham & Straus would "have room enough to take care of all their business for some time to come."[31] By 1896, Abraham & Straus employed more than two thousand workers. Store employees enjoyed many unique benefits and revolutionary labor practices. A ladies' lunchroom, employee roof deck, in-store doctor and nurse, free Thanksgiving turkeys and Saturday summer closings were examples of exclusive company perks.

Abraham & Straus grew to 600,000 square feet in floor space and rivaled some of the country's most prominent department stores in terms of size and sales. A *Brooklyn Daily Eagle* editorial noted, "New York has produced a Stewart, Philadelphia a Wanamaker and Brooklyn an Abraham, for it is due to Mr. Abraham's genius and indefatigable energy that the great business of Abraham & Straus has developed….It is a store that embodies all the latest ideas in store management that has in operation many ideas that originated in the store itself and have since been adopted by other stores….Brooklyn now has a modernized store and a retail establishment unrivaled by any in the United States and that means in the world, for America leads the world in store architecture and store keeping."[32] A new home delivery system, which included a fleet of 239 horses and 130 wagons, served customers far beyond its Fulton Street trading area.

Although they were invested in Abraham & Straus, Isidor and Nathan Straus focused most of their attention on R.H. Macy & Company. All three Straus brothers were heavily involved in politics and the Democratic Party. Nathan was a candidate for New York mayor and served as the New York City parks commissioner and the president of the New York Board of Health, Oscar was a United States secretary of commerce and labor and Isidor served New York's Fifteenth Congressional District as its United States Representative.

The Abraham family largely stayed away from politics and concentrated their energies on store operations and community service. Abraham's sons-in-law, Simon F. Rothschild and Edward C. Blum, played active roles in the management of Abraham & Straus. Rothschild married Abraham's daughter Lillian, and Blum married daughter Florence. Simon F. Rothschild focused on the store's constant physical expansion needs, and Blum focused on merchandising. In 1903, Blum established Abraham & Straus's European buying office and severed the store's operational ties with R.H. Macy & Company. Despite the competition between the two stores, the Abraham and Straus families were close and frequently socialized. Abraham Abraham and Nathan Straus owned twin summer homes on Cherry Island in New York's Thousand Islands.

In 1897, Brooklyn, the nation's third-largest city, was home to 3.1 million citizens. Its constant expansion was the result of massive waves of immigration and impressive industrial growth. City services were taxed as Brooklyn's finances and government became financially overwhelmed.[33] New York City residents pressured Brooklynites to abandon its status as a separate city and join New York as a borough. The combined real estate created in New York City the second-largest city in the world, outside of London. On January 1, 1898, the Charter of Greater New York was signed, and Brooklyn joined New York City as its fifth borough.

Abraham Abraham supported the consolidation of Brooklyn into New York City. Abraham ultimately believed that "the merger would make a stronger Brooklyn."[34] He saw the consolidation of Brooklyn into Greater New York as an opportunity similar to the building of the Brooklyn Bridge: "As to the future of Brooklyn as I see it now—it is as boundless as its magnificent territory and splendid situation.…With improved transit facilities, [New York] will build up a world metropolis which will leave London behind."[35] Abraham backed up his statement with two more expansions to his Fulton Street landmark store. In 1900, a warehouse was erected along Livingston Street, and additional Hoyt Street frontage was completed two years later.

With more than 4,600 employees, Abraham & Straus was the largest store in the city and state. Its horse-drawn delivery system was replaced with "horseless automobile delivery wagons" in 1895. The new wagons delivered approximately forty-five thousand packages daily to various roadside "agencies" throughout Brooklyn and Long Island—from Riverhead to Islip, Rockaway Beach, East Hampton, Sag Harbor, Patchogue and more. These "distributing stations" remained in operation throughout the 1920s. In 1899, a storewide telephone system was established that simply used the Brooklyn exchange "12." The enormity of Abraham & Straus defined Greater New York's growth. The *Brooklyn Daily Eagle* reported, "Volumes might be written about the store of Abraham & Straus but no adequate conception of the immensity of the establishment and the wealth of goods there offered for sale can be had until one visits the place and pays note to the interior arrangements and fittings and the stock itself. Truly, Abraham & Straus have the model store of this greater city, and one of which the firm may well be proud."[36]

CHAPTER 4

Keeping Up with the Strauses

*Samuel Rothschild and Edward Blum built a business that Brooklyn beloved….
At Abraham & Straus, customers knew that a yard wasn't 35½ inches.*
—*Walter S. Rothschild, December 1, 1953*

B y the early 1900s, department store competition had intensified throughout New York City. On November 8, 1902, R.H. Macy & Company, under the leadership of Isidor Straus, opened a massive new store at Broadway and Thirty-Fourth Street. With twenty-four acres of sales space, Macy's was billed as the "World's Largest Store."[37] Philadelphia's John Wanamaker, Chicago's Marshall Field and Detroit's J.L. Hudson also competed for this top honor. The new R.H. Macy & Company store surpassed Abraham & Straus as New York's largest store, but Abraham & Straus continued further expansions. In 1905, Abraham & Straus purchased the ground rights along Livingston Street, from Hoyt Street to Gallatin Place; expanded its basement store; and increased the building by 100,000 square feet.

A new Brooklyn subway system inaugurated service on May 4, 1908. The subway provided quick and essential passenger service to Manhattan, the Bronx and nearby Long Island towns. Involved in its early discussions, Abraham Abraham urged that the new subway converge in the Fulton Street area and create a downtown Brooklyn transportation hub. Abraham & Straus designed an elaborate Hoyt Street subway station that featured a direct entrance into the store's basement. Large display windows were installed in the Hoyt Street station. Its private subway entrance became the first such private entryway throughout the entire New York subway system.[38]

On the subway's opening day, the Hoyt Street ticket booth, located at the Abraham & Straus basement entrance, sold more than five thousand five-cent tokens. Abraham & Straus reported, "[The subway opening] was a tribute to Brooklyn…crowd[s] came to see Abraham and Straus, and to buy, because of the unmatchable values.…It was gratifying to know that these visitors exclaimed not only over the remarkable values, but over the beauty of the store itself and its subway entrance. Bronx is but a few minutes away now and this is an attractive entrance to Brooklyn, a doorway worthy of the borough destined to be greatest in the city." Abraham praised the new subway and its effect on Brooklyn: "Things certainly have changed since I began my business career in Brooklyn—and they have changed for the better in every way. Nevertheless, remarkable as have been the changes in this borough, rapidly as this section of the greater city has increased in population and importance in recent years, I am satisfied that the development has only just begun and the changes in the next ten years will be even more startling than they have been in the past."[39]

Abraham Abraham passed away at his Thousand Islands summer home on June 28, 1911. His unexpected death was diagnosed as being from acute indigestion that led to cardiac failure. Abraham's sons-in-law, Simon Rothschild and Edward Blum, immediately left their Bayshore homes for Thousand Islands. The news of Abraham's death stunned employees. The store closed for five days as the employees and customers mourned his passing. A short typewritten notice was posted at the store's main entrance. The *Brooklyn Daily Eagle* reported, "The relations between [the store's employees] and Mr. Abraham had been deeper than those which usually obtain between an employer and his employees."[40]

Abraham was one of Brooklyn's most charitable and visible citizens. He served as a board member for the Brooklyn Institute of Arts and Sciences, the chamber of commerce, Temple Israel, the Jewish Hospital, Hebrew Orphan Asylum and the Federation of Jewish Charities. On December 11, 1911, a large memorial was held at the Brooklyn Academy of Music's Opera House. Attendees and dignitaries praised Abraham for championing "every cause" made for the civic, social and industrial progress of Brooklyn, along with his powerful political insistence for "clean government" officials. In an editorial, the *Brooklyn Daily Eagle* noted, "All Brooklyn mourns him as one whose place may never, in a strict sense, be filled."[41] Following Abraham's death, Simon F. Rothschild,

Edward C. Blum and Simon's son, Walter Rothschild Sr., assumed executive leadership of the department store.

On April 15, 1912, Isidor and Ida Straus embarked on the maiden voyage of the RMS *Titanic*. After the *Titanic* collided with an iceberg and began to sink, Ida Straus was urged by crewmembers to join women and children in a lifeboat. Ida refused to leave her husband's side, and the two succumbed in the disaster. The death of Isidor Straus rocked R.H. Macy & Company and the New York business community. In addition to his management at Macy's, Isidor was regarded as one of the city's greatest philanthropists. Abraham & Straus employees composed a message to the Straus family that memorialized the Strauses and acknowledged the horrible loss. The letter expressed the employees' sorrow and showed appreciation "not only of the lesson of their lives, but of the beautiful inspiration in their death....We indeed extend our sympathy to the family of Mr. and Mrs. Isidor Straus… but we also feel that no heritage could be so everlastingly sublime as the memory of the nobility of the death of this man and woman."[42]

Isidor's death left a leadership void at Macy's. Jesse, Percy and Herbert Straus, sons of Isidor, had been actively involved at Macy's and served in many executive positions. Nathan's sons, Hugh Grant and Nathan Jr., were working their way up Macy's corporate ranks. Hugh Grant and Nathan Jr. wanted more control in the business decisions at Macy's, but Jesse, Percy and Herbert refused to advance their cousins into the executive corps. They did not feel that their cousins were ready and able to hold leadership positions. A corporate fight divided the Straus family. In November 1913, Nathan Straus announced his retirement from R.H. Macy & Company and sold his interest in Macy's to Isidor's sons. In return, Isidor's sons relinquished their investment in Abraham & Straus in addition to the L. Straus & Company china and glass import business. After the Macy's and Abraham & Straus investments were divided between the cousins, the two families ended all communications. Hugh Grant Straus joined Simon F. Rothschild and Edward C. Blum as managerial partners at Abraham & Straus. His brother, Nathan Straus Jr., elected not to work at Abraham & Straus and pursued a career in publishing and political causes. Their father, Nathan Straus Sr., continued as a managing partner at Abraham & Straus but devoted most of his time to humanitarian causes.

Throughout the 1910s, Abraham & Straus maintained its stature as the second-largest store in the New York Metropolitan Area. Abraham & Straus employed almost six thousand workers and housed more than twenty-eight acres of space. The department store offered many unique features for its customers. A street-level fountain, arranged like a bar with a full-time attendant, offered free drinking water. A complete food department offered essential and gourmet products. Many of the food items were sold under the store's in-house *Priscilla* label. A&S manufactured its own line of candies, drugs and toilet goods and processed its own coffee and tea. Catering to Brooklyn's ethnic diversity, the department store employed interpreters in twenty-three different languages, from Gaelic to Hebrew, Dutch, Slavic, Syrian, Armenian and German. Female employees were encouraged to take special arithmetic, spelling and writing courses taught by Brooklyn public school teachers.

By 1900, large department stores could be found in most American cities. Historian Jan Whitaker stated, "[Department stores] set a new standard for the way the consumer should expect to be treated, the type of services that should be provided for free or at minimal cost, and the convenience that should attend the process of acquiring the necessities and niceties of life all in one place. In short, they made shopping into a leisure pastime."[43] Numerous department stores of varying sizes opened up, and competition increased throughout New York City. In 1896, John Wanamaker established a large operation at Ninth and Broadway, the site of the former A.T. Stewart Company. Stewart, a mentor of Wanamaker, was often credited as the country's first "Merchant Prince" and founder of the American department store. In 1910, department store competition further intensified as Gimbel Brothers opened a large ten-story store just one block south of Macy's Herald Square location. Gimbels successfully ran department stores in Milwaukee and Philadelphia but wanted to take advantage of New York's consumer buying power. Both Macy's and Gimbels had strong financial resources that funded building expansions. Both stores were located in the heart of Manhattan, where many subway lines converged. Nearby stores such as B. Altman & Company, Lord & Taylor, Hearn's, McCreery's and Saks Thirty-Fourth Street store created New York's premier and most powerful shopping district. Although it was popular in Brooklyn, Abraham & Straus worked hard to convince shoppers to cross the East River and shop at its Fulton Street location. It remained competitive and attracted customers throughout the city, but Abraham & Straus dropped to third place in sales and size among New York City's department stores.

As competition intensified in Manhattan, Abraham & Straus planned "a building program that would take care of the needs of a city whose development has been so phenomenal as to be almost incredible, whose future possibilities are without limit."[44] In order to achieve these goals, the

By 1939, R.H. Macy & Co.'s Herald Square store contained 2,012,000 square feet and enjoyed the largest daily traffic of any store in the world. Macy's housed 168 individual departments of merchandise.

company transitioned from a business managed by multiple partners to a corporation run by a board of directors. On February 1, 1920, Abraham & Straus filed paperwork and became Abraham & Straus Inc. Company partners became shareholders, and a new structured board of directors was formed. Nathan Straus Sr., Simon F. Rothschild, Edward C. Blum, Lawrence Abraham, Lee Kohns (Nathan Straus's nephew), Hugh Grant Straus and Walter N. Rothschild Sr. served on the company's first board of directors. The company's real estate holdings were spun off into a separate corporation, Abrast Realty Company.

In 1920, Abraham & Straus increased its buying power and joined the Associated Merchandising Corporation (AMC). Founded in 1918, AMC was able to purchase merchandise in discounted bulk quantities and then distribute items to member stores at a lower cost. Located in different geographical regions, AMC member stores did not directly compete with one another but rather exchanged data, advertising techniques, personnel training and other operational methods. AMC assisted stores with efficient operations and "helped its members become better stores." The Brooklyn department store knew that it had to remain competitive and innovative in order to "continue the traditions of the founders—of integrity, service, and progress."[45]

Chapter 5

The Store Accommodating

The Greatest Store and the Greatest Business in Brooklyn have arisen here on the foundation of Public Satisfaction, with the best service and the lowest prices, always linked with high quality.
—Abraham & Straus company creed, 1907–20

After the establishment of its new corporate structure, Nathan Straus was elected to chairman of the store's board of directors. Although he was named store chairman, Straus focused less on Abraham & Straus and more on his philanthropic causes. "The more his business activities expanded, and the greater his commercial success, the keener did he see and feel the misfortunes of the poor," noted the *Brooklyn Daily Eagle*. Straus was regarded as "a world famous philanthropist, benefactor of the sick and poor in many lands, champion of Zionism, and dean of American Jewry."[46] Abraham's son-in-law Simon Rothschild was elected president and assumed managerial leadership of the store.

As Simon became more active and visible with civic causes, the Rothschild name became synonymous with Abraham & Straus. Simon Rothschild founded the Brooklyn Federation of Jewish Charities and the Downtown Brooklyn Association. He also served as a director of the Brooklyn Academy of Music. The Rothschilds had no relation to the powerful Rothschild bankers in Europe. Walter's grandson Walter (Trip) Rothschild III recalled the story when his grandfather met one of the French Rothschilds in the 1920s. Walter Rothschild Sr. was asked, "What branch of the [Rothschild]

An advertisement from July 7, 1927, states that the Abraham & Straus Subway Store features low prices but not at the sacrifice of quality.

family do you belong?" Walter replied, "The Brooklyn branch [in reference to the department store]."

On October 8, 1923, Abraham & Straus opened its "A&S Subway Store," home of Brooklyn's Best Bargains. Described as a "Store Within a Store," the A&S Subway Store sold lower-priced clothing of dependable quality. The store promised "the same policy of liberality" that had made Abraham & Straus a respected retail leader. It provided a generous return policy, a "homey" atmosphere, charge account privileges and free delivery. The Subway Store "relieved [the departments located upstairs] of certain lower price lines" and permitted the upper floors to "develop these departments in scope and efficiency hitherto impossible."[47] In addition to the Subway Store's opening, Abraham & Straus modernized its main floor and installed escalators from the basement to the fourth floor. Supervised by Vice-President Edward C. Blum, Abraham & Straus embarked on additional renovations that included a new cold storage facility, an ice refrigeration plant and a sanitary bedding factory.[48] Employees were offered conveniences such as a smoking room, roof garden, library and store choral society. By 1924, Abraham & Straus had swelled to 800,000 square feet and four thousand employees.

Abraham & Straus marked its sixtieth anniversary with an elaborate display window that looked sixty years into the future. The display depicted the store as a "skyscraper in an area of skyscrapers, with Fulton Street [as] a double-decked highway supporting omnibuses instead of trolley cars on its surface and consigning to a lower level delivery trucks and other vehicular traffic of today. The store proper [was] represented as having upon its roof a landing field from which airplanes are continuously taking off [and making] deliveries in this country, and a mooring mast from which swings a dirigible for more distant deliveries, including transatlantic."[49] During a January 1925 anniversary dinner, Vice-President Edward C. Blum stated, "We all know that in education the three R's stand out as fundamental. [For the] fundamentals in business I would [use] the three H's: Highmindedness, human-mindedness, and horse sense."[50] In December 1925, Abraham & Straus announced an initial $4.25 million public stock offering that funded future modernization and expansion plans. By 1925, annual sales had increased from $2.5 million in 1886 to more than $24 million. The department store's preferred and common stock made its debut on the New York Store Exchange on February 25, 1926.

Nathan Straus Sr. retired as chairman of the board in December 1925. Straus had not been active in the store for many years.[51] Upon Nathan's retirement, Simon F. Rothschild assumed Abraham & Straus's top position. His son, Walter N. Rothschild Sr., was named general manager two years later. Simon worked tirelessly and improved internal employee relations. He encouraged buyers to make independent decisions within their designated departments and not rely on input and approval from store executives. In 1927, Simon Rothschild established an Executive Training Squad, which recruited college graduates and offered current employees the opportunity for corporate advancement. Abraham & Straus's leadership team scouted trainees with "character, stamina, brains, plus a good education." The Executive Training Squad members learned all facets of the department store business, from selling to buying. "Eventually you can become what you are good at. It may be a buyer, an administrator, or a coordinator," stated a divisional merchandise manager in an A&S employee publication.[52] Abraham & Straus's revolutionary Executive Training Squad became a model program throughout the country's department store industry.

In 1927, Abraham & Straus opened the Anscot Shop at 54 Court Street in Brooklyn's new "skyscraper district." Billed as the "exclusive outfitters to gentlemen," the Anscot Shop featured two floors of "society brand clothing" surrounded by rich oak paneling, leather furniture and a Gothic-influenced interior design. On December 30, 1928, Vice-President Edward C. Blum announced a total rebuilding project of the Fulton Street landmark. A brand-new, very large Abraham & Straus store was designed to be built in three stages. The first phase included a fifty-five-foot strip that connected Fulton Street with Livingston Street, along with some frontage along Hoyt Street. Exterior plans featured an eight-story limestone and granite façade.

In 1929, Abraham & Straus became a founding member of Federated Department Stores. A 1943 *Annual Report* displayed images of its earliest member stores. Stores shown, *clockwise from far right*: Abraham & Straus, Brooklyn; Lazarus, Columbus; Filene's, Boston; Bloomingdale's, New York; R.H. White's, Boston; and Shillito's, Cincinnati.

An ornate bank of twelve passenger elevators and a "battery of escalators" facilitated customer traffic within the new structure. The installation of indirect lighting addressed complaints by shoppers who demanded improved merchandise visibility.

Famed commercial architects Starrett & Van Vleck drew up plans for the new Fulton Street store. Starrett & Van Vleck architects traveled to several European cities and studied the latest commercial construction techniques and brick patterns. The finalized designs were the result of a ten-year study that analyzed growth on Fulton Street and the entire borough of Brooklyn. Construction of the first phase began in early January 1929, and business was never interrupted during the rebuilding period. The first phase was completed in just ten months, from January to October 1929, and expanded the department store to 1.2 million square feet. Extra care was used to match floor heights that had shifted over time. Phase One was officially completed on October 10, 1929, but further development soon ground to a halt. In just a few short weeks, the New York Stock Exchange experienced its historic crash.

Back in February 1929, leaders of Boston-based Wm. Filene's Sons Inc.

A 1929 advertisement in *Brooklyn Life* depicted the anticipated uniformly designed Abraham & Straus department store. The company only completed the first of its three stages of reconstruction due to Depression concerns.

and Abraham & Straus began formal discussions about a merger between the two stores. One month later, the two department stores announced the creation of a central holding company. The merger's mission was to bring "unified control to successful retail stores through their acquisition and affiliation."[53] Store vice-president Walter N. Rothschild and Filene's vice-president, Louis F. Kirstein, led the efforts between the two stores. The planned merger helped address unfounded rumors that R.H. Macy & Company had planned an acquisition of Abraham & Straus. Columbus-based F. & R. Lazarus & Company, along with its sister division, Cincinnati's John Shillitto Company, were invited to join further discussions.[54]

On March 29, 1929, Abraham & Straus executives Simon F. Rothschild, Edward C. Blum, Hugh Grant Straus and Walter

N. Rothschild notified Abraham & Straus shareholders of the formation of a new retail holding company and asked shareholders for their support. A letter to Abraham & Straus's common shareholders asserted that the department store consolidation "increased operating efficiency and growth in volume and profits."[55] Company executives stated that one share of Abraham & Straus would be exchanged for one and a half shares of new stock under the name Federated Department Stores Inc.

Leaders of Abraham & Straus, Filene's and Lazarus, along with Paul Mazur from Lehman Brothers, gathered on Walter Rothschild's yacht and finalized the details of the new Federated Department Stores firm. Simon Bloomingdale accompanied the store leaders on the Long Island Sound cruise. Federated was designed to be a holding company of member stores that operated individually and not under one corporate umbrella. The cooperation and support between its members was designed to help offset potential risk if any member store suffered financial losses.[56] Federated encouraged its members to belong to the Retail Research Association and the Associated Merchandising Corporation.

On November 25, 1929, official paperwork was filed in Wilmington, Delaware, and Federated Department Stores was officially incorporated. Abraham & Straus, Filene's and Lazarus were charter members and were soon joined by Bloomingdale Brothers. A. Lincoln Filene was named Federated's new chairman of the board, and Simon F. Rothschild was named company president. The timing of Federated's incorporation proved essential, as the country was soon thrown into economic and social depression.

CHAPTER 6

Fulton Street at Hoyt

After several years of consistent and impressive gains, the New York Stock Exchange crashed in late October 1929. Within a matter of days, thousands of investors lost billions of dollars. By 1933, approximately 30 percent of American workers faced the unemployment lines. The economic collapse struck fear throughout the public and private sectors. As 1929 came to a close, Abraham & Straus maintained an optimistic outlook. Simon Rothschild insisted that the company was "fundamentally sound," and sales figures surpassed those of the previous year. Rothschild assured investors, "The conditions we find in our own business at the present time are, we believe, an index of the general economic status. There are few more accurate barometers of the economic conditions of a country than the retail store."[57] The affiliation with Federated Department Stores provided a sense of security at Abraham & Straus. The company decided to halt all future construction plans and eliminate any current financial risk. Years later, as the country's economy improved, Abraham & Straus never restarted its grand rebuilding program from early 1929.

In 1930, Edward C. Blum assumed the presidency of Abraham & Straus. The husband of Florence Abraham, Blum wanted to operate the store while upholding "the ideals of the founder." No store employees lost their jobs during the Depression, but all workers agreed to a 10 percent salary cut to be "restored as soon as conditions permitted."[58] In January 1930, employees established a Mutual Benefit Association. Association members paid dues that provided funds in case of sickness or accident. Health and life insurance,

On May 16, 1938, Abraham & Straus opened an appliance store at 168–04 Jamaica Avenue, Queens. The building included a model kitchen and a one-hundred-seat basement auditorium for special events.

along with emergency loans, were later added to the MBA program. During the 1930s, Abraham & Straus adjusted employee schedules to coincide with store traffic count and accommodate schedule requests.

In 1931, Abraham & Straus established the first in-house department store photography studio when famed photographer Herman Mishkin relocated his New York studio to the Brooklyn building. Best known for his work at the Metropolitan Opera, Mishkin photographed more than 100,000 persons. On December 3, 1934, Abraham & Straus expanded beyond downtown Brooklyn and opened a household appliance store in Jamaica. Located at Hillside Avenue and 166th Street in Queens, the Jamaica branch sold oil burners, automatic refrigerators, gas stoves and washing machines. Abraham & Straus anticipated a high demand for these household products, as the Federal Housing Act loan program had earmarked $5 million for home improvement loans in Queens. Throughout the 1930s, sales figures remained strong at Abraham & Straus, but the story was different at its parent firm. Federated Department Stores posted consistent sales declines, which included a 19 percent drop between 1931 and 1932. Sales figures at Federated finally stabilized in 1935, and the parent company experienced measured and modest growth throughout the rest of the decade.

Simon F. Rothschild passed away on January 5, 1936, at age seventy-five. Active in numerous charities throughout the area, Simon was one of the original four partners who had formed Abraham & Straus in 1893. Simon's death created a shift within A&S's corporate structure—Edward C. Blum was named chairman of the board, and Walter N. Rothschild,

ABRAHAM & STRAUS PRESENTS ELEPHANT
TO REPLACE HILDA IN BROOKLYN ZOO

Park Commissioner Moses Accepts
Offer Made on Behalf of Brooklyn's
Grieving Children

On September 15, 1938, Abraham & Straus donated a baby elephant to the Brooklyn Zoo. The new elephant replaced the popular pachyderm "Hilda," which was reportedly injured while playing with another elephant. A&S offered a naming contest for the new elephant. Its new name, "Astra," derived from the store's name, was selected and announced the following month.

Simon's son, became store president. Visible in the community and admired by his peers, Walter Rothschild was an active and beloved figure at Abraham & Straus. Joseph Kasper, a former executive vice-president at R.H. Macy & Company, worked alongside Walter during his time at the store. Kasper resigned from Macy's in 1944 and became president of the Associated Merchandising Corporation. In 1953, Kasper reflected on Walter's leadership at Abraham & Straus: "[Walter] is not only a great person or a great citizen, he is just one great damn swell fellow.… He has tremendous pride in the heritage that was handed down to him. When an individual happens to be related to the founder, he could have chosen anything out of retail but [Walter] preferred to accept the responsibility of the heritage of this great store. He has added new goals that those who follow him will have to live up to and succeed." Walter's grandson, Walter (Trip) Rothschild III, recalled his grandfather as "jolly and warm." He credited his grandfather for operating a store that was open to customers from a variety of economic and social backgrounds: "Abraham & Straus seemed like some great melting pot of ethnicities."

As the nation slowly recovered from the Depression, Abraham & Straus strengthened its community and employee relations programs. In October 1938, the department store made a highly publicized addition to the Prospect Park Zoo. Abraham & Straus donated a baby female elephant to the zoo's pachyderm exhibit. The department store sponsored a contest for Brooklyn schoolchildren and solicited names for the baby elephant. Astra, a simplified variation on the store's name, was selected. Other finalists included Sweetie Pie, Flat Foot, Floogie and Roberta. Astra was unveiled at "one of largest and most socially correct gatherings, except for a slight stampede of 13,000

Abraham & Straus kicked off its seventy-fifth anniversary Jubilee celebration on February 1, 1940. This image shows the main floor of the original 1873 building.

children."[59] Astra was a fixture at the Prospect Park Zoo until June 1958, when she was euthanized for aggression.

In 1939, Mrs. Edward C. (Florence) Blum, the A&S chairman's wife, organized an effort that adopted the forsythia as Brooklyn's official flower. Brooklyn borough president John Cashmore signed a resolution that "encouraged" Brooklynites to make their "front yard[s] blaze with yellow beauty when blossom time comes around." Forsythia Day was an annual Brooklyn event, and its founding was often credited to Mrs. Blum. In 1940, a Forsythia Day celebration message read, "Forsythia, our Brooklyn official flower, sends you and the world its friendly message of Brotherhood, Unity, and Understanding."[60] In April, Abraham & Straus's fifth-floor garden center frequently featured elaborate forsythia displays designed by various area garden clubs. Forsythia Day has continued to be an annual Brooklyn event, often sponsored by the Brooklyn Botanic Garden.

As the store built up its community relations policy, it also strengthened its internal relationships among its workforce. Abraham & Straus's benefit

This photograph shows the Abraham & Straus Brooklyn store from the intersection of Livingston and Hoyt Streets.

programs continually evolved and expanded to include a three-week vacation policy, Blue Cross health coverage, time-and-a-half overtime pay and the first such retirement plan to be offered in a New York City department store.

During 1940, Abraham & Straus counted 12 million customers who visited the Brooklyn store, with 7 million "wrapped" packages; 6 million bags and 2.5 million boxes were distributed for store purchases. The department store employed 2,400 full-time workers at the Brooklyn store, 624 of whom had been with the company for ten years or more. Annual sales reached $24.3 million, and employee wages totaled $3.8 million.[61] In March 1940, a newly designed Basement Store opened that featured a new level of "pleasant" fluorescent lighting. A&S provided several dining options for its customers. Shoppers could dine in the full-service fifth-floor restaurant, have a simple lunch in the first-floor Priscilla Shop or grab a quick snack or custard parfait at the basement lunch counter. The Fulton Street store also housed an extensive prescription drug and liquor department, an ice cream and candy factory and a testing laboratory for merchandise, as well as a card room, gymnasium, hospital and employee library. With more than 1 million square feet of sales space, Abraham & Straus welcomed an average of 70,000 visitors each day.

This image shows the Fulton Street Elevated Line as seen outside the downtown Abraham & Straus. This view is from the intersection of Fulton and Duffield Streets. *Courtesy of the Percy Varian Photograph Collection, v1987.10: Brooklyn Historical Society.*

The Fulton Street Line's structure was removed in 1941 after the outcry of many area merchants. This view shows the removal of many supports to the rail line structure, from the intersection of Fulton and Lawrence Streets. *Courtesy of the Percy Varian Photograph Collection, v1987.10: Brooklyn Historical Society.*

World War II posed new challenges for the country's department store industry. Many male employees left their jobs for their country. More than 220 "A&Sians" served in the armed forces, and their absences created employee shortages at the department store. A&S promised that all employees assigned to active duty would have their jobs waiting for them upon return, along with a financial bonus. The remaining workers were offered a $2.50 bonus for any new recruit they referred for employment. A&S employees helped spearhead six local war loan drives that raised tens of millions of dollars, along with several Red Cross blood drives. During 1944, store employees made approximately nine hundred blood bank donations. The Abraham & Straus Women's Volunteer Corps was a prominent organization established during the war. Members of the Volunteer Corps donated clerical services to the Office of Civilian Defense, worked on fuel rationing programs and learned fingerprinting techniques. The corps also organized social events at the Manhattan Beach Coast Guard Station and Fort Hancock.

Brooklyn's Fulton Street Elevated Train Line dated back to April 1888 and had long cast a shadow over Brooklyn's center core. The outmoded train cars

On June 26, 1947, Walter Rothschild Sr., Borough President John Cashmore, Mrs. Howard Nieman and R.E. Blum cut the ribbon on the new Livingston Street addition.

In 1951, Abraham & Straus supported the federal government's newly enforced guidelines on price-fixing. In this photograph, hundreds of toothbrushes are deeply discounted. The department store advertised that fair pricing is not a new policy.

"screeched and groaned" on the dilapidated elevated structure, often referred to by Brooklynites as the "Black Spider."[62] On May 31, 1940, the antiquated train line ended its service. The next day, thousands came to Fulton Street and watched Mayor LaGuardia apply an oxy-acetylene torch to the rambling structure. Over the next several weeks, curious onlookers lined Fulton Street amid showers of sparks and angry work machines. The remains of the steel structure provided three thousand tons of scrap material for American defense needs. One Fulton Street shop owner exclaimed, "We'll be able to have a little sunshine now!"[63] With the absence of the elevated structure, Fulton Street proponents promised a shopping district that could rival any in appearance, including Manhattan's Fifth Avenue. Merchants, including Abraham & Straus, pledged more than $3 million of improvements to their Fulton Street façades and entryways. Brooklyn's downtown shopping district enjoyed a rebirth. From 1941 to 1948, annual sales at Abraham & Straus increased from $24 million to more than $64 million.

On June 9, 1946, Abraham Straus announced, "Happy Birthday, Dear Breuckelen," in honor of the borough's 300th anniversary.

Edward C. Blum, store chairman and son-in-law of founder Abraham Abraham, passed away on November 20, 1946. Edward's son, Richard, had served as store vice-president and secretary, but the leadership torch was passed to Walter N. Rothschild Sr. Sidney L. Solomon had joined Abraham & Straus in 1934 as the basement merchandise manager but was soon promoted to vice-president and general merchandise manager. In March 1948, Rothschild named Solomon general manager of the Brooklyn department store, as well as a corporate vice-president of the board of directors. Solomon was the first Abraham & Straus executive hired outside of the founding families.

After the war ended, Abraham & Straus expanded its frontage along Livingston Street and opened another addition on June 25, 1947. A team of horses traveled down Livingston Street on its opening day. When the horses arrived at the store's new Livingston Street entranceway, a lady dressed in "feathers and fluff" handed a golden key to Mrs. Howard S. Nieman, one of the store's oldest customers. The eighty-thousand-square-foot addition included a special events center that catered to store and community organizations. President Walter N. Rothschild Sr. told reporters that the Livingston Street building "constitutes a public expression of faith in the bright future of Brooklyn."

During its construction, Abraham & Straus executives initially feared that rising costs, increasing material shortages and a possible economic recession would hamper the expansion efforts, but those fears were never realized. Luckily, postwar optimism and beautification efforts brought continued economic hope and development to the Fulton Street shopping corridor. Upon the opening of the Livingston Street addition, a *Brooklyn Eagle* editorial noted, "Brooklyn is blessed with many progressively minded citizens, merchants as well as others….Brooklyn should be proud of Abraham & Straus. The development of the downtown section, through its civic center, its improved shopping district and eventually its rehabilitated residential areas, is materially advanced by the kind of leadership this great establishment has shown."[64]

CHAPTER 7

Downtown Shopping Center

There's a new thrill of neighborhood pride in the air…
A stepped-up tempo to the everyday business of selling and shopping…
And such a flurry of face-lifting, painting, and polishing
You haven't seen on Fulton Street in years.
—Brooklyn Daily Eagle, *advertisement, November 4, 1953*

Outside Midtown Manhattan, Brooklyn was New York's largest shopping district. Abraham & Straus dominated the Fulton Street corridor, but it was not the only large retailer that called Brooklyn home. In the 1940s, a Fulton Street beautification effort included the elevated train removal and storefront modernizations. The elimination of the Fulton Street elevated train brought a fresh and bright image to the formerly darkened street. In 1941, the *Brooklyn Daily Eagle* praised Fulton Street: "Thronged with shoppers, the new Fulton St. is symbolic of the progressive Brooklyn of Today—and the Brooklyn of Tomorrow."[65]

Located directly across from Abraham & Straus, Martin's was one of downtown Brooklyn's largest stores. Martin's did not function as a complete department store but rather offered quality merchandise and personalized service spread throughout its many floors. Martin's and Abraham & Straus did not directly compete with each other, but their different styles, offerings and price points complemented each other and helped make busy Fulton Street a true retail destination. In 1966, *New York Times* columnist Isadore Barmash called Martin's an "oasis of calm, even understatement" amid the "din of traffic and shopping hub-bub" on Fulton Street.[66]

Located at the corner of Fulton and Bridge Streets, Martin's was founded in 1910. In 1916, Hyman Zeitz purchased the modest dress shop from its original owners and continually grew the business, expanding into several adjoining buildings and acquiring the seven-story Offerman Building in 1925. Hyman Zeitz passed away in 1930, but his family remained active in the store's management. In 1932, a Subway Store, which offered discounted and off-price merchandise, was opened in Martin's basement floor. Martin's Subway Store operated through much of the 1930s and accounted for almost one-third of the business's total sales during the Depression. The Zeitz family played an active role in the 1940 removal of the Fulton Street elevated train.

By the early 1960s, Martin's was operating branches in Huntington, Babylon and Garden City and posting $25 million in annual sales. The 225,000-square-foot Brooklyn flagship boasted $15 million of that total. In 1966, Wilbur A. Levin, former Martin's president, told the *New York Times*, "Our appeal must remain based on fashion and service, not on price, although we are mindful of this factor and don't want to bury our head in the sand."[67] Martin's eventually added a menswear department but never expanded into home goods. Despite a number of acquisition attempts, Martin's remained a privately owned business. The Zeitz family operated Martin's throughout most of its existence, and the store was known as one of the country's largest family-run specialty retailers.

Founded in 1860, Frederick Loeser & Company was one of Abraham & Straus's strongest competitors. Often regarded as Brooklyn's carriage trade department store, Loeser's was "a vital cog in the string of department stores and big specialty shops" in Brooklyn's Fulton Street retail district.[68] In March 1888, Loeser relocated his lower Fulton Street store and joined Wechsler & Abraham in the new shopping district. Commercial architect Ernest Alan Van Vleck designed Loeser's signature building, located at Fulton and Bond Streets. Van Vleck was part of the same architectural team that worked on Abraham & Straus's 1929 rebuilding project.

In 1934, Loeser's became the first Brooklyn retailer to open a suburban branch location. The small Garden City store, located at Ninth Street and Garden Avenue, quickly exceeded all sales expectations. On May 16, 1937, Loeser's opened an enlarged Garden City store that featured forty thousand square feet of selling space, seventy-five departments and parking for several hundred cars. Loeser's three-story building "provided Nassau County and Long Island [with] a shopping center equaled by few, if any, in the whole country."[69] In June 1940, Frederick Loeser & Company continued

It's big news for Brooklyn . . . a story with a happy ending! Two famous names that grew up with Brooklyn now become one, to carry on the tradition of almost a century of service . . . 76-year-old Namm's and 92-year old Loeser's.

Namm's is proud and happy to announce that we have acquired from Loeser's its fine old store name, good-will and trademarks —and we are immediately changing our firm name to NAMM-LOESER'S . . .

Namm's has acquired Loeser's branch store in Bayshore, Long Island, located at 108-112 East Main Street, and will continue to operate the Bayshore Branch of Namm-Loeser's with the same competent organization which has been serving that community for the past eleven years.

Loeser's charge and budget customers can now pay their outstanding accounts at our 11th floor credit office. Also, Loeser's gift certificates and coupon books can be redeemed in any of our Namm-Loeser's departments.

We look upon this as a great opportunity to add new glory to our long history of contribution to the famous Fulton Street shopping center, as well as to enable us to continue to play an ever longer part in Brooklyn's growth and welfare.

We know that Loeser's customers, as heads of other Brooklyn people, will find shopping easy and pleasant at Namm-Loeser's . . . on our brilliantly, newly lighted modern street floor . . . our streamlined fashion second floor . . . in our many modernized third floor linens, fabrics, curtains, lamps, toys, pet shop . . . enlarged fourth floor housewares, floor coverings, huge china and glassware sections . . . our vast famous-for-values fifth floor furniture and bedding departments . . . and in our Thrift Basement.

Yes, Namm's has kept in step with the times, and we are ever growing, with more bigger and better plans for the future. We pledge ourselves to continue to render to the people of Brooklyn and Long Island the same conscientious, outstanding service for which both Namm's and Loeser's have so long been noted . . . to offer you quality merchandise of top brand names, honest values—in an ever-widening variety.

On March 9, 1952, Namm's announced the acquisition of the Frederick Loeser Brooklyn store. Benjamin Namm declared the purchase and the continuation of the Loeser name as "A Story with a Happy Ending." Namm-Loeser's subsequently closed in 1957.

its suburban expansion and opened a branch in Bay Shore, Long Island. Located at 108–112 East Main Street, the Bay Shore store focused primarily on women's apparel.

Despite its suburban branch development, Loeser's remained committed to its downtown Brooklyn location. In 1940, Loeser's completely modernized its first two floors and installed the country's largest fluorescent lighting system. The new lighting provided "a radiant brightness—brilliant and clear as the light of a Summer noon."[70] After the war, management and ownership changes plagued the company. In September 1950, Frederick Loeser & Company sold its profitable Garden City store to Abraham & Straus. Loeser's president told the *Brooklyn Eagle*, "The action was taken as a step in the development of the policy of the new owners of Loeser's to concentrate on increasing the sales volume of its store in Brooklyn to its full potential."[71] However, the sale was not enough to stabilize the company's finances.

On February 8, 1952, Loeser's announced that its large downtown Brooklyn flagship would close. Six days later, approximately 20,000 shoppers surrounded all three sides of the building for its final sale. Police and fire crews worked endlessly to control the crowds. The escalator power was shut off when shoppers were unable to step off the moving stairway without stumbling over one another. After the store's liquidation ended, 1,200 employees, represented by eight separate unions, lost their jobs. The closing of Loeser's concerned other downtown Brooklyn merchants. Benjamin H. Namm, operator of Namm's department store and Loeser's next-door neighbor, told reporters, "It is most regrettable that Brooklyn's oldest department store, and one of its greatest landmarks, is finally going to liquidate after almost 100 years of noteworthy and faithful service."[72] Benjamin Namm urged city officials to study the collapse of Loeser's and "render a constructive report to the Brooklyn public."

In 1876, Benjamin Namm's father, Adolph, founded the A.I. Namm & Son store in Manhattan. Located at Sixth Avenue and Eighteenth Street, the Namm building was sold to Benjamin Altman in 1886. After the sale to Altman, Adolph relocated his business to Brooklyn. In 1925, Namm opened a new eight-story building that was dubbed "a triumph of retailing."[73] Namm's featured a Bargain Basement that eventually included its own direct subway entrance, along with Brooklyn's first escalator. The 500,000-square-foot store advertised "quality merchandise, top brand names, [and] honest values in an ever-widening variety."[74]

On March 9, 1952, Namm's purchased the name and goodwill of the recently closed downtown Loeser store, in addition to its suburban Bay Shore location. The company immediately changed its name to Namm-Loeser's. President Benjamin Namm felt that the Loeser name had value and that Loeser's had "always been considered one of the finest department store names in the entire country."[75] Namm-Loeser's continued its Long Island expansion and acquired Milk's, a small department store located in Woodmere, in November 1952. Namm-Loeser's also announced plans for a large suburban branch at the new Lake Success Shopping Center on Union Turnpike. The Lake Success store was never built, and rumors circulated that the company was in trouble. Word spread that the business was underperforming and that Benjamin Namm wanted to retire. By the mid-1950s, Namm's annual sales were less than half of its 1920 figures, and the company's future seemed tenuous.

For many decades, Oppenheim Collins was a downtown Brooklyn mainstay. Charles Oppenheim was the son of Albert Oppenheim and Mary Abraham, sister of A&S founder Abraham Abraham. Charles along with his father, Albert, worked alongside Thomas Collins at Wechsler &

On March 10, 1954, hundreds swarmed A&S's Brooklyn basement store for its "Sale of Sales." One bargain table featured items for four cents or less.

Abraham. In 1875, the Oppenheims and Collins left Wechsler & Abraham and established a wholesale business on New York's Canal Street. In 1901, the men opened its first retail ready-to-wear apparel shop at Broadway and Twenty-First Street. The store quickly grew in popularity and moved to Thirty-Fourth Street.[76] In addition to Manhattan, the company opened locations in Philadelphia and Buffalo.

On October 25, 1906, Oppenheim Collins expanded into Brooklyn with a store at Fulton and Bridge Streets. The popular Brooklyn location carried primarily women's and children's apparel throughout four selling floors. With the financial backing of its parent company, City Specialty Stores, Oppenheim Collins expanded throughout the Northeast with locations from Baltimore to Connecticut. In the New York region, Oppenheim Collins operated stores on Manhattan's Thirty-Fourth Street, Garden City, Huntington, Bay Shore, Hicksville and several New Jersey locations.

In September 1956, Oppenheim Collins sold its Fulton Street lease to E.J. Korvette, one of America's fastest-growing discount retailers.

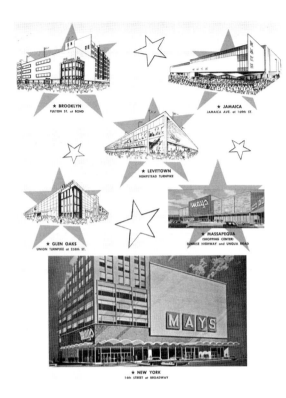

By 1963, the popularly priced JW Mays Company included locations in downtown Brooklyn, Jamaica, Levittown, Glen Oaks and Massapequa, along with a new large Manhattan branch at Fourteenth Street and Broadway.

Korvettes, founded in June 1948, was an aggressive retailer and a pioneer in discounting hard goods. Store founder Eugene Ferkauf named his store by using his first initial, his friend Joseph Zwillenberg's first initial and the small Canadian warship *Corvette*, a favorite of Zwillenberg's.[77] Ferkauf was "gratified" to locate in downtown Brooklyn and "enter the fray of big-time competition for the first time." Ferkauf saw Abraham & Straus as "the most profitable, most respected department store in America." Abraham & Straus president Sidney L. Solomon expressed "regret in losing an old neighbor in the departure of Oppenheim Collins" but was happy to welcome Korvettes, "who will bring even more customers into the downtown Brooklyn area."[78] As Korvettes opened its downtown Brooklyn store in May 1957, A&S officials told the *New York Times*, "[A&S] was prepared to meet [Korvettes on] all competitive prices on advertised merchandise."

Another popular Brooklyn department store was JW Mays. Mays, founded in 1924, grew from a tiny dress shop to a seven-story, 300,000-square-foot apparel store that encompassed an entire city block. Store founder Joseph Weinstein named his business after his favorite season in addition to his initials. At Mays, the slogan was "Every Day a Sale Day." Mays purchased

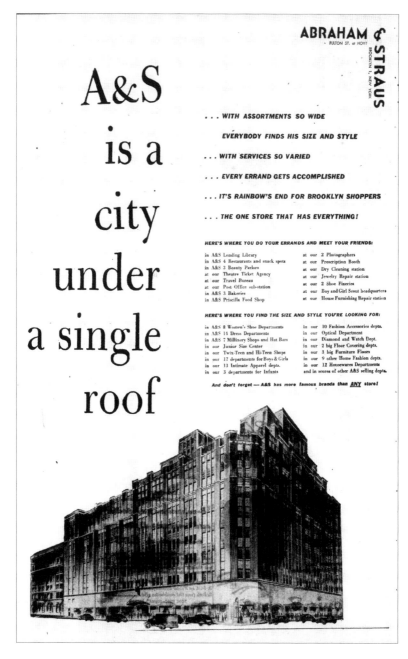

As the Hempstead A&S prepared for its 1952 debut, Abraham & Straus published an advertisement in the *Brooklyn Eagle* that reminded customers of the power and variety of its Fulton Street flagship. A&S declared, "It's Rainbow's End for Brooklyn shoppers, the one store that has everything. And don't forget—A&S has more famous brands than ANY store!"

the vacant Frederick Loeser store in April 1952 and increased its downtown Brooklyn footprint. Weinstein wanted to "maintain the character of Fulton Street and the volume or retail business done there."[79]

On August 26, 1954, the new Fulton Street Mays opened and was dubbed the "World's Largest Fashion Store." Mays addressed the demands of its suburban customers and expanded into Queens and Levittown. Weinstein stated, "The Fulton Street area is one of the most important shopping and mercantile centers in metropolitan New York. As a businessman with an important interest in the area, my principal objective in this purchase was to protect the high retailing standards of Fulton St. and to make certain that any future occupancy of the premises would maintain these standards."[80] In 1954, Brooklyn's downtown retailers promoted Fulton Street's revitalized shopping corridor. The borough felt confident in the area's economic future, despite an exodus of residents who transplanted to Nassau County and other area towns. As Fulton Street celebrated its status as New York's second-largest retail district, merchants inaugurated a popular advertising campaign that simply asked, "O say, have you seen the streamlined 'new look' in Brooklyn's major Downtown Shopping Center?"

CHAPTER 8

Suburban Sprawl

Abraham & Straus is as much a part of Brooklyn as the Dodgers. When Brooklynites moved to the suburbs, they usually moved to Long Island. When A&S decided to open branch stores, it moved to Long Island where the people by tradition already liked to shop at A&S.
—*Federated Department Stores* Annual Report, *1955*

After the war, merchandise shortages ended as factory production lines refocused on civilian goods. As soldiers returned from duty, housing shortages gave way to suburban residential expansions. The population explosion helped grow "America's productive capacity and contributed to a rise in discretionary income."[81] Single-family home construction exploded throughout Long Island. Builder William Levitt purchased thousands of acres of land near the town of Hempstead. Between 1946 and 1951, Levitt & Sons constructed more than seventeen thousand homes in a new planned community named Levittown. Levittown, New York, "became a national symbol for suburbia during the post World War II building boom."[82]

When Loeser's decided to sell its Garden City store, located approximately seven miles from Levittown, Abraham & Straus seized the opportunity. On October 2, 1950, Abraham & Straus Garden City officially opened for business. With approximately eighty thousand square feet of sales space, the three-story location was relatively small and did not offer the full selection of merchandise found at the Brooklyn flagship. Local Nassau County shoppers

On October 1, 1950, Abraham & Straus acquired Loeser's Garden City store. The smallest of all future branch locations, A&S Garden City focused largely on apparel and was expanded to eighty thousand square feet in 1956.

welcomed A&S since many local residents were eager to purchase necessities closer to home. Long Islanders grew tired of long shopping excursions to Brooklyn, Queens and Manhattan. The Garden City Abraham & Straus store opened to "an eager and expectant public" and quickly built a "highly successful business with a large clientele."[83]

The village of Hempstead was one of the fastest-growing areas in the country, and its environs were ripe for commercial growth. More than 2.3 million Long Islanders lived within a short drive to the Nassau County community. On December 28, 1950, A&S announced that it would construct a full-service department store in the village. Designed by the French brutalist architect Marcel Breuer, A&S featured "a smooth, inviting façade, dimpled brick, corner entrances and windowless walls." Its location was "deliberately removed from the main business district…but in the direction of [Hempstead's] probable growth."

Store manager Walter Rothschild Jr., son of the company president, opened the Hempstead A&S on February 28, 1952. A grand opening advertisement stated, "Tomorrow for the first time in Nassau County, homemakers will find the complete selections of merchandise available only in large metropolitan shopping areas....Located in Hempstead at the very hub of Long Island, a cinch to reach us by car or bus, you'll find A&S Nassau truly 'A great store nearer home!'" A&S Hempstead carried "all departments found in the main Brooklyn store [and offered] customers the best of city service in the suburbs." The store exceeded all sales expectations, and by 1959, a third and fourth floor had been added. At 560,000 square feet, A&S Hempstead became "the largest suburban department store in the Northeast." A&S president Walter Rothschild Sr. affectionately called the Hempstead store "Little Gargantua."

A&S Hempstead was not intended to replace the smaller Garden City location. In contrast, the Garden City store catered to an established, fashion-oriented customer. The Garden City and Hempstead stores were located only three miles apart but enjoyed a friendly and competitive rivalry. Their rivalry was showcased at a celebratory dinner that honored store president Walter Rothschild Sr.

On December 1, 1953, Rothschild received accolades for his forty years of leadership at the department store. More than five hundred executives and industry leaders gathered at Brooklyn's Towers Hotel. Vice-President

Abraham & Straus Nassau dominates the shopping center of Hempstead. The insert shows a section of the spacious parking lots.

The Austin Company, the designer and builder of A&S Hempstead, described the new store as "ultra-modern in concept, from its four corner entrances to the beautiful 40-foot mural of Long Island in the 180-seat restaurant." Austin's design permitted free-flowing customer movement in the shopping areas and free-flowing merchandise handling in the storage and traffic areas."

Left: A&S Hempstead opened for business on February 28, 1952. The department store stated that "homemakers will find the complete selections of merchandise heretofore available only in large metropolitan shopping areas."

Below: The popular Hempstead A&S expanded to three floors in December 1954, less than two years after its February 1952 grand opening. The addition increased the store's selling area by more than one-third.

Sidney L. Solomon served as the evening's emcee, poking "affectionate satiric fun" at Rothschild and the company. Garden City vice-president Mel Westmore and Hempstead vice-president Turner Davies sang a parody based on the song "Anything You Can Do, I Can Do Better." The new lyrics read, "Anything you can sell, I can sell better. I can sell anything better than you." Garden City sang, "Say have you noticed our smooth elevators," to which Hempstead replied, "We have the same escalators to boot." Davies continued, "We have a beauty salon out in Hempstead," to which Westmore replied, "Our girls don't need one they're already beautiful." One final verse by the Garden City's vice-president stated, "My store sells to classes, that's why it's the fastest," as Hempstead answered, "My store sells to classes and the masses!"

At the dinner, Garden City managers presented Rothschild with a lifetime pass for the Long Island Railroad between Brooklyn and Garden City, without stopover privileges in Hempstead. Hempstead store manager Walter Rothschild Jr. jokingly commented, "We at the Hempstead store, as you might as well expect, have felt a heavy responsibility. It became increasingly evident during the past 1¾ years that we owe the Brooklyn store the correct type of leadership. So we made available to them our excellent advice, as we have been accustomed to doing in every aspect of the business....[My father] has been particularly interested in details. He has always offered us many suggestions and we have followed one or maybe two of them." By 1953, the Brooklyn, Garden City and Hempstead Abraham & Straus stores posted record-breaking annual sales of $100 million. Among the ten divisions of Federated Department Stores, Abraham & Straus claimed more than 22 percent of the parent firm's annual sales.

At the anniversary dinner, former A&S secretary Jack Little praised Walter's accomplishments and devotion to A&S. "Born with an illustrious name, which in itself signifies dignity and authority, [Rothschild] has handled his business with nothing but dignity. Courage. Fortitude." Little stated that Federated Department Stores wanted to build the Hempstead at only half of its completed size but that Rothschild convinced Federated otherwise. "People have respect for [Rothschild's] opinions and respect for his judgment."

At the evening's conclusion, Rothschild addressed the audience and told attendees that it had been a wonderful forty years and that, with "considerable pride," he had seen the business grow. Rothschild discussed his grandfather Abraham Abraham, along with the early days of the business. He praised the past and present commercial and civic leadership

Abraham & Straus is often credited as being one of the earliest retailers that brought humor into its advertising. In the 1940s and 1950s, Barney Tobey, a frequent contract author for the *New Yorker* magazine, produced a series of advertisements for the department store.

efforts by members of the Rothschild and Blum families. Rothschild concluded, "We do not ever want to rest on our laurels in this business. I'm sure that we're going to continue to grow and I'm sure we're going to advance our business in just the same fashion that we've built in the past. I'm very grateful to you for what you've given me tonight. And in return, all I can say is you've got my admiration, my appreciation, and my affection." Walter Rothschild Sr. remained president of Abraham & Straus until 1955. He retired from store management and served as board chairman until his death in October 1960. A *New York Times* tribute stated that Walter "provided over a store with a heart" and that "New York benefited by having Walter Rothschild in its midst."[84]

Walter's grandson, Trip Rothschild, said that "it was the natural role of department store founders to become civic leaders and A&S worked with the [Brooklyn] community more than most businesses." In 1951, Abraham & Straus initiated its Junior Angler Fishing Contest for area boys and girls. With the cooperation of the New York City Department of Parks, children ages sixteen and under engaged in a four-week fishing competition at Prospect Park Lake. The annual event attracted thousands of young Brooklynites, who competed for prizes for the heaviest, longest, largest number and first and last fish caught.

The A&S High School Board held monthly meetings for young women interested in the latest fashions. Composed of girls mostly from Midwood, Lincoln, Girls, Staubenmiller, Jackson and Textile High Schools, the board provided a social outlet for its high school members and communicated popular local fashion trends to A&S buying staff.[85] A&S also sponsored a two-year scholarship at the Tobe-Coburn School for Fashion Careers. The program included on-the-job experience at the department store. Children of A&S employees with three years or more of service were eligible for college scholarships based on financial need. Community children's programs sponsored by the department store included monthly "Star Gazers" meetings held in conjunction with the Amateur Astronomers Association, a Junior Achievement troop, the A&S Brooklyn Blades Junior Ice Skating Competition and children's exhibitions on rocketry, nuclear energy and other current scientific topics. On June 24, 1954, A&S donated $2,500 to establish a penguin colony at Coney Island's new aquarium.

On October 9, 1957, Abraham & Straus opened a location at Babylon's new Great South Bay Center. Located thirty-five miles from its Brooklyn store, A&S Babylon was the company's first venture into Suffolk County. At the time of its opening, Suffolk County's year-round population had blossomed to more than 412,000 residents. The new Babylon store promised "Big City Shopping" and everything for everybody "from teaspoons to a Tall Girls' Shop, from bicycles to a Bridal Shop, from diamonds to a Do-It-Yourself Shop, [and] from mirrors to a Maternity Shop." Parking for eight hundred automobiles and a "stunning" restaurant helped make the new store a retail destination. A&S Babylon was located just a few miles from the new Gimbels Bay Shore, a modestly sized former Namm-Loeser's acquired by Gimbels in March 1957.

One of five New York City–based department stores to join the retail graveyard in the 1950s—including Frederick Loeser & Company (1952), McCreery's (1953), John Wanamaker (1954) and Hearn's (1955)—Namm-Loeser ceased operations and sold off its stores in 1957. In addition to the Bay Shore store being purchased by Gimbels, its downtown Brooklyn building was purchased by Abraham & Straus. A&S demolished the former

In 1956, A&S presented an artist's rendering of its planned Babylon store in a company newsletter. A "complete" store, A&S Babylon, at the Great South Bay Center, was increased to three floors in 1962.

Namm-Loeser structure and constructed a new six-hundred-car parking garage in its place. Completed in 1959, the new parking facility included a ground-floor annex store that carried major appliances and a third-floor covered walkway into the main store, along with additional office space. The project was groundbreaking, as it contained the first parking facility built and utilized by a major downtown department store in all Manhattan and the five boroughs.[86]

In the early 1960s, many American department stores looked beyond their downtown locations for future plans. A 1961 *Women's Wear Daily* article reported, "Many downtown stores have branched into the suburbs to revive their sagging vitality. But if the parent store suffers from 'tired blood,' how can the branches be expected to have anything but 'tired sap'?" The trade publication stated that Abraham & Straus's Brooklyn store was one of the few exceptions: "Such an accusation could not be hurled at Macy's Herald Square or Abraham & Straus in Brooklyn. Each of these stores sponsors a host of institutional events during the year as essential supplements of aggressive merchandising and sales promotional procedures. In consequence, Macy's and A&S have been able to retain their number one and two positions both for main store and total-area volume."[87]

A new annex, built in 1959 on the site of the former Namm-Loeser's store, included customer parking, new selling space and expanded offices. An underground tunnel and bridge connected the annex with the main store.

A *Federated Department Stores Annual Report* declared, "If a community grows, retailing grows." A fourth floor was added to the Hempstead store in 1959.

In a 1961 Federated Department Stores *Annual Report*, Federated acknowledged that a growing number of suburban customers demanded greater convenience in shopping closer to home. Federated stated, "Suburban living creates a demand for new kinds of merchandise....[Federated has] to provide the goods and services that potential customers want, when they want them, and as they want them." In September 1962, Abraham & Straus joined

Store president Sidney L. Solomon and Chairman Walter N. Rothschild Sr. overlook the Brooklyn store's street floor in 1958.

Macy's at the new Walt Whitman Shopping Center. It was the first instance when Abraham & Straus and R.H. Macy & Company directly competed with each other in the same shopping complex.

Located in the Suffolk County Town of Huntington, the $20 million Walt Whitman Shopping Center was the New York area's first enclosed shopping mall. A&S's Walt Whitman store promoted "enormous assortments from the world's leading manufacturers, all the latest fashions from the designers you love, the famous-for-generations A&S services (including a charming restaurant and snack bar), a wide variety of credit plans to ease every budget and season and unbeatable discounts on famous brands." Shoppers at the new shopping center "walked through the mall's wide doors from shop to shop in the 70 degree temperature....They admired the Japanese gardens, sculptures, and the brilliant plumage of tropical birds in a gilded aviary."[88] The 220,000-square-foot Walt Whitman A&S utilized the slogan, "The Great Store Nearer Home!" and boasted that "more Long Islanders shop at A&S than at any other store."[89]

The massive Hempstead store offered 3,000 free parking spaces for customers, which included a 1,200-space tiered parking garage.

A large branch at the Walt Whitman Shopping Center opened on March 28, 1962. The 220,000-square-foot location featured a large, colorful mural that depicted an early Abraham & Straus roadside agency over the store's main entrance.

Across the country, department stores did not always create a welcome shopping environment for African Americans. In many instances, African Americans were unable to use fitting rooms or return merchandise. Dining facilities were often off limits, and African American shoppers were relegated to the basement selling floors. Abraham & Straus had a reputation as one of the more "open" department stores for African Americans in the New York Metropolitan Area. "A&S was far more in touch with civil

In 1965, the company's *Spotlight* magazine featured a collage of all five Abraham & Straus stores.

rights [than other stores]," stated family member Trip Rothschild. "They prided themselves on it. A&S welcomed African American shoppers which was perceived as progressive." In 1963, Federated Department Stores, A&S's parent firm, told shareholders, "We need to have the kind of courageous sensitivity that will make us willing corporate participants in the great human struggles of our century—be they the nation's quest for peace or the Negro's legitimate aspiration for equality." Federated was the country's first major retailer to sign up with President Kennedy's "Plans for Progress," a voluntary program for companies that pledged extra efforts at job opportunities for African Americans.

By the 1960s, Abraham & Straus was the fifth-highest revenue producer of all American department stores. At more than 1.6 million square feet of space, its Brooklyn flagship was the third-largest department store building in the country and the second-largest in New York City, behind Macy's Herald Square. Since 1952, it had enjoyed consistent annual sales gains. A&S's five locations provided more than 3 million square feet of floor space for Brooklyn and Long Island shoppers. As the department store approached its 1965 centennial, Chairman Sidney Solomon and President Walter Rothschild Jr. looked forward to continued success and a bright future.

CHAPTER 9

A&S Loves You

The last century has been a one hundred year love affair between A&S and the public. The customers are thrilled and exasperated, confiding and critical. They laugh at us and swear at us, and learn from us and thankfully buy from us.
—William Tobey, A&S vice-president of sales promotion,
1965 company statement

Abraham & Straus officially celebrated its 100th birthday on February 15, 1965. Deputy Borough President John Hayes presented a "scroll honoring the store's contribution to the economic well-being of the community and support of civic, humanitarian, and cultural activities in Brooklyn" to Walter N. Rothschild Jr. In recognition of its centennial, Abraham & Straus renovated the Hoyt Street subway station with fresh coatings of yellow and turquoise paints, new benches and bright chandeliers. Customers were showered with "A&S Loves Me" buttons and treated to complimentary sirloin steak lunches.[90] The *New York Herald Tribune* reported that "there were enough 'A&S Loves Me' pins to supply every little boy in Brooklyn." Nine thousand company employees received specially engraved key rings that acknowledged their years of service and "helping [the store] reach 100."

In honor of the milestone, Abraham & Straus announced the construction of a new Children's Zoo at Prospect Park. Built and maintained by the Department of Parks, the exhibit featured a "barn, paddocks, duck pond, a covered bridge, silo and tree house, along with domestic animals and baby animals to pet. [It was] the only such rural

A company postcard displayed the official design for the company's 100th anniversary image and slogan, "A&S and You: A Hundred Year Love Affair."

experience available to young city slickers." President Rothschild stated, "Soon after my great grandfather opened his store in 1865, he inaugurated a tradition of interest in the children of Brooklyn according to the greatest needs of the city. Now we think that an old-time Dutch farmyard with animals to pet, should be a good and needed diversion for children growing up in the largest metropolitan complex in history."[91] An anniversary brochure reflected, "Before Abraham Abraham died in 1911 at the age of 68, he had realized his dream…for he and his associates had succeeded in giving a great community that great department store it richly deserved. The management of A&S and its employees today, constantly strive to maintain and further the policies set forth by the store's founder, Abraham Abraham."

During its centennial year, Abraham & Straus purchased twenty-three acres of land at Northern Boulevard and Community Drive on Manhasset's Miracle Mile. The property was home to the two-hundred-year-old Mitchill homestead, one of the last remaining examples of eighteenth-century architecture on Long Island. A&S relocated the Mitchill house to North Hempstead and cleared the land. On May 6, 1965, the new Manhasset A&S 262,000-square-foot branch store joined other prestigious New York retailers such as Lord & Taylor, Arnold Constable, Bonwit Teller and B. Altman & Company along the upscale "long entrenched" shopping strip. The *New York Times* noted, "In what may be a Joshua-like effort, Abraham & Straus will attempt to break down the walls of Jericho.…The walls that Abraham & Straus will be trying to break down will hardly be Biblical, but will be the competitive walls that have prevented the company from not doing more business in Northeast Queens and the Northwestern part of Nassau County."

Manhasset customers desired "higher-priced merchandise to meet constantly improving consumer tastes."[92] Although the Miracle Mile was well-stored, A&S Manhasset was the strip's first full-line department store.

"That whole stretch of the Miracle Mile housed all of the 'cream-of-the-crop stores' and A&S's treated its Manhasset store like it was a flagship," said former associate Scott Snyder. Mel Wilmore, A&S vice-president, recalled that the Manhasset store "had the highest quality clientele." The patrons were "very demanding," stated former director of stores Curtis Champlain. "Customers would park right at the curb in Manhasset. We also had a high amount of returns. Some customers returned clothes they obviously wore." With its latest success at Manhasset, A&S's annual sales swelled to $220 million in 1965.

Although it was committed to further expansion, Abraham & Straus remained dedicated to its downtown Brooklyn flagship. Its 1959 annex building, home to the store's parking garage and appliance department, was expanded to include additional sales space. An extra floor increased the building's size to 1,593,000 square feet. Executive Douglas A. Schuler recalled the Brooklyn store as "a very powerful, dominant factor. It was huge and did lots of business. It was a gem which had some beautiful Art Deco areas." Schuler stated that going to Fulton Street "was a big event. You didn't have the type of stores in Brooklyn that they had in Manhattan."

A&S also provided a sense of culture and tradition for its customers. "You walked in the store and the first thing you saw was the elevator bank. It was so beautiful," said Curtis Champlain. "People had no problem talking to the elevator operators. Everybody got a wonderful greeting. And if I ever wanted some inside information, I'd ask the elevator operators. [I learned:] Do not talk in an elevator!" In a 1979 interview, elevator supervisor Leon Scott described Christmastime on Fulton Street:

During its centennial year, Abraham & Straus opened a location in Manhasset on May 6. The popular Manhasset store was located in the heart of Long Island's surging population and commercial growth.

In this holiday season, let us all join in a prayer for peace on earth and for the well being of our servicemen in the troubled parts of the world.

We at A&S are about to complete another banner year of sales and service to our Brooklyn and Long Island communities. All of our stores have had another fine year of growth. You have also seen a considerable amount of very attractive refurbishing this year in our constant efforts to improve presentation of our colorful merchandise.

All of this was made possible by your sincere and friendly attitude of customer service of which I am genuinely proud and appreciative. I thank you for your hard work and fine enthusiasm, and wish you and yours a joyful Christmas and a happy New Year.

Sidney L. Solomon
Chairman of the Board

Left: In 1965, A&S chairman Sidney L. Solomon offered its associates a Christmas prayer for "peace on earth" and "the well being of our servicemen in the troubled parts of the world."

Below: A blurred photograph shows A&S's street floor during its 1965 centennial celebration.

People came from Pennsylvania, Connecticut, and other places just to see our decorations because they were different from any other store. Busloads of kids came to see Fantasy Land. Lights and candy canes and snowflakes trimmed the walls. It was a beautiful sight to see. Angels were placed on the post columns in the main floor lobby and the elevator courts had little toys and gifts for children to buy. Fantasy Land was decorated in a hazy blue just like a dream land and it was done with garlands and lights.

Abraham & Straus placed a large Christmas tree in the elevator court lobby that reached from floor to ceiling. "But we had problems with the tree," said Scott. "People used to walk into it if they were walking backwards or talking to someone." Leon Scott worked as an elevator operator for more than thirty years. A&S executives felt that elevator operators helped create a warm personal atmosphere at the store. Scott recalled, "I've heard people say 'Thank heavens they still have operators at A&S!' It enhances our business."[93]

"[In the 1960s,] the people [who managed] A&S were juggernauts," recalled former buyer Valerie Capobianco. "They were incredibly talented people. The buyers were legends in the industry. When they walked into a showroom, everything stopped. They couldn't do enough for A&S people." A 1967 Federated Department Stores *Annual Report* stated, "Success in our kind of business requires more than talent: it requires a particular quality of character." The A&S Executive Training Squad developed into one of the retail industry's most prestigious programs. Trainees accepted into the program received intensive instruction on all types of managerial, buying and selling functions at the business. Capobianco recalled, "I had complete stars in my eyes at my first orientation class. I hung on every word. One of the executives said that we may be referred to as a 'Beast of Burden.' He wanted to give us a dose of reality. Retail was not going to be all glamor. You just absorbed everything, from observing it to doing it."

Capobianco did not attribute all of the store's success to its executive talent. "Some of the employees on the floor were non-executive assistants who never wanted to take the full step into management. Some of these gals were some of the smartest, sharpest, hardest working people; part businesswoman, part mother. They were like mothers to the trainees, buyers, and customers. They were the salt of the earth!" Capobianco added that there was "no glass ceiling for women" at A&S. Mary Jane Solino served a long tenure at Abraham & Straus and said, "At A&S, the mantra was 'Take Care of the Customer.' The customers made A&S great." *New York Times*

A company postcard depicts the revolving Christmas tree in the Brooklyn store's elevator court, an annual tradition.

A 1965 company telephone directory listed all six A&S's locations.

retail columnist Isadore Barmash detailed the store's atmosphere during the late 1960s: "With its success marked by canny price-hustling and fashions targeted to its solidly middle-class clientele, A&S could boast of the department store industry's highest net income, $30 million. Its management was probably best regarded in the retailing field and its sales help was warmly referred to by shoppers as 'those nice, nice people.'"[94]

Downtown Brooklyn was not immune to many of the economic and social issues that swept the country during the 1960s. Large public housing projects "threatened" the downtown strip and created "a big shift in the area's ethnic and income population." Increased competition within the borough challenged the traditional Fulton Street retail district. In July 1967, a large E.J. Korvette department store opened in Brooklyn's Bath Beach neighborhood. On October 8, 1968, ground was broken on Kings Plaza, a new shopping and marina complex located at Flatbush Avenue and Avenue U. Macy's, Alexander's and one hundred additional stores joined Kings Plaza in New York City's first enclosed shopping mall. Both retail centers offered free parking and late night shopping hours, in contrast to downtown's crowded streets and sidewalks. "The winds of change, some balmy, some sharp-edged, are bearing down on Fulton Street," reported the New York Times.[95]

While some people feared that increased competition could signal the possible demise on Fulton Street, many local leaders felt that continued urban renewal efforts in downtown Brooklyn offered economic security. The popularity of Abraham & Straus, Martin's and Mays helped secure the district as a citywide shopping destination. All three large stores appealed to a variety of customers. The massive A&S store offered a vast selection of merchandise and Mays presented affordable apparel, while Martin's carried fashionable, higher-end goods. Martin's also sold more bridal gowns than any other business in the country.

In 1969, A&S continued its expansion efforts and joined Macy's at the new Smith Haven Mall, located on Route 25 between Smithtown and

Men's merchandise at the Fulton Street A&S was frequently situated on the store's large mezzanine. The name "London Shop" was often used for the men's suit department. *Courtesy of the Frank Nieves Jr. Collection.*

Brookhaven. Located in one of the country's fastest-growing areas, the large 1.4-million-square-foot Smith Haven Mall was more than sixty miles from A&S's downtown Brooklyn flagship. "When I joined Abraham & Straus, I called Smith Haven our Midwest store," said former director of stores Curtis Champlin. "All of the shoppers wore jeans and pushed baby carriages. It was like our country store. The customers prided themselves in never visiting New York City." In 1969, A&S also opened a furniture and mattress store in Carle Place, a hamlet in North Hempstead. Carle Place also served as a warehouse store for the department store. "It didn't do much business and acted as kind of a dumpster," remembered Champlin.

The year 1969 also marked the end of an era, as President Walter Rothschild Jr. resigned from A&S. Rothschild was the last Abraham family member who worked in store management. Rothschild decided to leave the department store and devote his time to community service. His commitment to social programs emulated service of past members of the Abraham family. "My father wasn't that satisfied with the business," said

In May 1969, Abraham & Straus went head to head with Macy's at the new Smith Haven Mall. *Courtesy of the Copeland, Novak & Israel International Collection.*

Martin's, as seen in this Smith Haven Mall image, frequently located its suburban businesses near A&S branches. *Courtesy of the Abbott, Merkt & Company Collection.*

Walter's son Trip Rothschild. "He became far more in touch with civil aspects than the retail industry. It was just a natural role for him to become a civic leader." Rothschild also realized that he would have to invest at least ten more years in order to become company chairman. "[My father] felt he didn't need to be chairman. Federated [Department Stores] had become a much more centralized company." During his tenure, Rothschild maintained Abraham & Straus's role as a community-minded company. Walter personally spearheaded projects such as street maintenance and sanitation, urban renewal projects and financial assistance for lower-income residents.

After his retirement at age forty-nine, Rothschild remained loyal to the department store. "I remember that my mother went to the Huntington A&S for some clothes but ended up going down the mall to Macy's and bought a coat. She caught such incredible grief from my father!" said Trip Rothschild. After Rothschild's departure, Sidney Solomon remained as company chairman well into the 1970s. As the 1960s came to a close,

Above and opposite: In September 1968, A&S presented "Italia Bellissima," a festival devoted to Italian art, crafts, industry and culture. These images feature a display window and the Fulton Street men's department during the Italian festival. *Courtesy of the Frank Nieves Jr. Collection.*

Solomon reflected on Brooklyn. "[Brooklyn] is a city of homes. People live here, regardless of where they might work. The neighborliness of Brooklyn is an established thing." In a *New York Times* interview, dress manufacturer Leonard Arkin said, "Everybody felt at home [at A&S]. Brooklyn people always swear allegiance to the store. It was never highfalutin'—but in a quiet way it always stood behind its things. It was first in our hearts—the whole family shopped together. We went there right through high school, until we moved away."[96] With 246 selling departments, the iconic Abraham & Straus firm rightfully earned its slogan, "Don't say you can't find it 'til you've shopped at A&S."

CHAPTER 10

Worth a Trip from Anywhere

After all, we're from Brooklyn. And when you come from Brooklyn,
you've got to be good.
—*Abraham & Straus, store advertisement, August 4, 1981*

I n 1970, Abraham & Straus's Brooklyn flagship store enjoyed its largest sales increase in store history. It was the twenty-second year of continuous sales gains at the Brooklyn location. In a company document, Ralph Lazarus, chairman of Federated Department Stores, referred to the Fulton Street A&S as "the country's third largest department store complex with unrivaled profitability."[97] Despite demographic, economic and social shifts that affected the store's immediate area, A&S remained bullish on its Brooklyn flagship. The department store's popular Opportunity Day sales events combined clearance merchandise and special purchases. Its annual June swimwear price break was a popular early summer promotion. "People would wait and line up at the doors to buy the swimsuit of their dreams," recalled Valerie Capobianco. "The swimwear would be on racks one-half the length of the sales floor."

One popular company-wide celebration was titled "A&S Italia Bellissima." Two hundred avant-garde Italian lighting fixtures, along with fourteen master craftsmen and a forty-eight-foot replica of the Sistine Chapel ceiling, filled the Brooklyn store and were presented with the cooperation of the Italian government. Replicas of the Trevi Fountain in Hempstead, Michelangelo's *Pieta* in Babylon and Donatello's *David* in Manhasset, along with espresso and pastry from Ferrara, added to the celebration.

A&S also introduced a new boutique named L'Africana, which featured African-inspired clothing for men and women. Nigerian designer Malcolm Arbita designed much of the clothing sold in L'Africana. Former associate Scott Snyder frequented A&S's record department. "Every week, A&S's handed out a foldout that listed the top 25 hits. It rivaled [the popular record department at] Korvettes." In 1970, Abraham & Straus, along with the Herald Square Macy's, offered a black Santa Claus as a customer option. Families with children were "ushered up to a wall low enough to preserve the remaining illusions of childhood….The parents could turn left or right toward the race of their choice." The choice of Santas was initially met with skepticism, but customers soon accepted the practice. Blumstein's Department Store in Harlem had been the only other New York City retailer that offered a black Santa Claus. When Mel Wilmore arrived at A&S as its new Brooklyn store manager, he remembered, "At Christmastime in Brooklyn, we had to hire two Santas, a black Santa and a white Santa. You would get white kids go to the black Santa and black kids go to the white Santa. You saw the kids and they really didn't care. That was kind of cool." In a *New York Times* interview, one company executive stated, "Although times are changing, the fact remains that Brooklyn is a powerful market, the sixth largest central business district in the United States. But to stay abreast of the customers' needs, we feel that stores must modernize, both physically and in fashion image."[98]

In March 1971, A&S expanded into New Jersey, a market dominated by Newark-based Bamberger's. A three-story, 285,000-square-foot store opened at the Woodbridge Center, joining Stern's, Ohrbach's and 117 smaller stores. A&S management had "high hopes" for its first New Jersey location and planned for Woodbridge to be the first of several stores throughout the Garden State.[99] The Woodbridge Center was in proximity to the popular Menlo Park Mall, anchored by Bamberger's, a division of Macy's. Abraham & Straus felt confident that it could successfully attract new shoppers and compete with Menlo Park.

The new Woodbridge store hoped to draw new Garden State shoppers and customers from nearby Staten Island who were familiar with the Abraham & Straus name. The spring 1971 A&S employee magazine, *Spotlight*, stated, "We look forward with great anticipation to the opportunity of representing Abraham & Straus for the first time in the New Jersey community and accept the challenge of earning for ourselves the merchandise reputation and customer esteem that have become the A&S trademark everywhere."

This page: A&S's first New Jersey store was located at the Woodbridge Center. Opened in March 1971, Daniel Schwartzman & Associates created its unusual angular design. A&S included a self-contained budget store in order to best compete with the state's many discount stores.

Abraham & Straus was not the first New York–based retailer that expanded into New Jersey. B. Altman, Gimbels, S. Klein, Lord & Taylor, Alexander's, Bonwit Teller and Bloomingdale's joined local New Jersey stalwarts Bamberger's and Hahne's, a division of Associated Dry Goods. After a successful opening at Woodbridge, customer interest subsided and sales figures fell. Former Woodbridge manager Mel Wilmore stated, "Once we figured out how to merchandise the store, we showed [A&S executives] how to really operate within the culture and success of Bamberger's." Within a short period of time, annual sales climbed 9 percent. After several mall expansions throughout the 1970s, Woodbridge Center claimed to be the largest shopping center in the Northeast, with more than 230 stores and 5 department stores.

On September 12, 1973, A&S opened a new store in the Rego Park section of Queens. Located at Queens and Woodhaven Boulevards, A&S joined Ohrbach's in a 600,000-square-foot enclosed mall designed by famed commercial architect Victor Gruen. The new complex was built in proximity to an existing freestanding Alexander's department store and Macy's signature "store-in-the-round" in nearby Elmhurst. Despite the competition, Ohrbach's president Robert J. Suslow claimed, "[The] density of the local population, the relatively high Queens income, and the existence of a center as large as the Queens Center appear to us to augur well for our new store."[100]

A&S opened its popular Queens Center store on September 12, 1973. Ohrbach's joined A&S at the Queens Center, along with seventy specialty shops and restaurants. The Queens Center was located less than one mile from Macy's famous Elmhurst "store-in-the-round."

A&S executives touted the Queens Center location, with four floors of "fresh fashions," a Basement Store and "A&S famous-for-over-a-century friendliness and complete service" as "so uniquely A&S." The Queens Center A&S was wildly popular from opening day. The 1979 *Spotlight* reported, "[The Queens Center store] is constantly abuzz with the kind of pace usually found in a city store." The new center drew from the adjacent Lefrak City complex, a planned office-residential community that included twenty eighteen-story apartment buildings. Opened in 1961, Lefrak City originally housed white middle-income residents. But by the late 1960s, Lefrak City had integrated and maintained a roughly 50:50 ratio of white and black residents. "The Queens store was in a densely populated area due to the rise of all of the apartment buildings," said former Queens manager Mary Jane Solino. "The mall was very easy to get to."

The Queens Center store siphoned business from Jamaica, New York City's third-largest business district and home to the flagship Gertz department store and a Macy's branch that dated from 1947. Queens Center also attracted customers who frequently traveled to Brooklyn and Manhattan for shopping excursions. The Queens Center A&S increased pressure on the company's sprawling Hempstead location. The nation's largest suburban department store, A&S Hempstead, experienced a noticeable shift in its demographic customer base and was concerned about storefront vacancies in the downtown area.

In October 1969, New York mayor John Lindsay proposed an ambitious renovation of the Brooklyn Fulton Street retail corridor. He wanted to reinvent Brooklyn's downtown as a modern commercial and residential hub. Mayor Lindsay's plan was received with skepticism, but he refused to abandon his idea. Four years later, Mayor Lindsay submitted a Fulton Street plan that transformed eight blocks into a new pedestrian mall. The $4 million project received support from many Brooklyn merchants. Martin's, a longtime carriage trade retailer in the area, was especially attracted to the new mall. Martin's image seemed dated and irrelevant when compared to the district's new urban-based customer. "Martin's was much more of a B. Altman–type retailer," recalled former buyer Valerie Capobianco. "It was extremely traditional and had very, very light inventories." By the mid-1970s, Martin's four suburban Long Island stores and sole New Jersey location well outperformed its downtown Brooklyn flagship. In anticipation of the new Fulton Street project, Martin's promised a full renovation of the downtown store. However,

In spite of the area's many shopping centers, the Paramus Park A&S was one of the company's top-performing locations. *Courtesy of the Scott Snyder Collection.*

over the next several years, the mall experienced a series of planning and design changes. The first phase was not completed until June 1977.

Abraham & Straus continued its march into New Jersey with a new large branch in Bergen County. In March 1974, A&S and Sears, along with 120 smaller stores, opened at the new Paramus Park shopping mall. Paramus was already home to several large shopping centers. When initially proposed, Paramus Park was met with opposition, particularly by residents dismayed with the area's already congested roadways. In addition, the community expressed outrage at the "miles of highway-sign blight and retail honky-tonk" along Routes 4 and 17. "Many shoppers come here from New York City because they want to avoid traffic," stated Councilman Paul J. Contillo. "Now we're so snarled that they're going elsewhere. We're defeating ourselves. We're in danger of losing our identity as a residential community. You have to stop somewhere."[101] County representatives reassured area residents that Paramus Park would be the last large shopping center to be built and introduced a resolution that barred future projects. A&S Paramus was one of the department store chain's top performers. "Paramus was a fabulous store," recalled former store director Mel Wilmore. "We treated it differently just as we treated Manhasset differently. [Paramus and Manhasset] had a totally different customer base than our other locations. These stores had to be much more upscale in order to make sure that we were competitive."

In 1974, Federated Department Stores hired Sanford J. Zimmerman as A&S chairman and Alan B. Gilman as company president. Zimmerman was the former chairman of St. Louis's Famous-Barr department store group, and Gilman was chairman of Sanger-Harris in Dallas. Federated was impressed with the customer response and sales figures at the Manhasset and Paramus A&S stores and ordered other locations to offer more upscale merchandise. Federated was convinced that a merchandise upgrade would increase customer traffic and improve the store's "middle-of-the-road" image. However, the upgrade confused the department store's loyal customers, and sales suffered. "A&S tried to be more upscale and fashion forward but it was a mistake," said former manager Mary Jane Solino. "They reached too far to compete with Macy's and it came at a cost. A&S worked well with lower to mid-moderate merchandise." Mel Wilmore recalled, "One of the problems is that some people wanted A&S to be something it wasn't."

Once praised throughout the department store industry for its exemplary Executive Training Squad, A&S soon experienced high managerial turnovers. After trainees completed the Executive Training Squad program, graduates frequently left Abraham & Straus for better jobs within the industry. "It's impossible to have consistency in a business when you have four CEOs in 8 years," stated Wilmore. Without consistent leadership and direction, profits eroded. By the mid-1970s, the once highly profitable Brooklyn and Hempstead stores were plagued with problems. Urban blight severely affected the Fulton Street neighborhood, and an economic downturn affected many Long Islanders, especially many longtime Hempstead customers. By the end of the decade, Abraham & Straus had lost its status as the most profitable division of Federated Department Stores.

Abraham & Straus was also burdened with theft rates that severely affected the company's bottom line. With impressive annual sales of $120 million, A&S Fulton Street posted a staggering 10 percent inventory shortage rate. Branch store shrinkage numbers added another $20 million to that figure. At the Brooklyn store, small gangs occasionally roamed the store and grabbed as much merchandise as they could before fleeing. During the overnight hours, dogs were placed at the store's entrances to help deter and catch criminals who had hid in the building after its evening closure. Former Fulton Street manager Mel Wilmore recalled the "unbelievable" scenes that traditionally occurred on Christmas Eve. "We used to close at 6pm but at 5:15, people would gang up outside and rush the store. They would spread out like ants and you could never watch them

In the mid-1990s, the store's signature Art Deco tower still sported the company's logo from the late mid-1970s.

all. Black, white, I'd never seen anything like it." A&S hired an additional fifty to sixty security guards on Christmas Eve.

Throughout the year, menswear and better dress departments traditionally experienced the highest theft rates. Former manager Curtis Champlin remembered, "Whenever somebody got caught [shoplifting], we'd have to take them to the police station but it reduced the [number of] security guards on the floor. Every day, we had more arrests than the 84th precinct!" Eventually, two jail cells were installed in the downtown Brooklyn store to detain shoplifters. After he became the Brooklyn store manager, Champlin focused on the store's internal and external theft rates. Champlin felt that a reduction in shrinkage numbers would be easier to obtain than an increase in sales volume. "It was the quickest way to make a profit." During his tenure as manager, Mel Wilmore controlled product placement throughout the store. Higher-priced merchandise was kept out of easy reach from potential shoplifters. "We determined what [merchandise] goes on a counter and what stays in the case. We stopped putting $200 bottles of perfume on top of the cases! In one year, our shrinkage rate dropped from 8% to 3½%."

As its immediate neighborhood deteriorated, shortages at Hempstead skyrocketed. Anti-theft programs were installed in all branch stores. Babylon associates organized a "Shortage Committee" that brainstormed solutions and kept associates updated with the latest anti-theft techniques. At the Queens Center A&S, "Police came by a couple times a day to take people to the station," said former manager Mary Jane Solino. "The NYPD set up a detail and trained staff on how to fill out DATs [desk appearance tickets] and fingerprint."

The store's proximity to the Lefrak City housing complex contributed to its shortage problems. "Lefrak City became the drug capital of Queens," said Solino. Easy access to the Woodhaven Boulevard subway station, located close to the Queens store, also contributed to its high theft rate. The higher-end Manhasset store was not immune to these issues. "There were professional thieves at Manhasset who had so many tricks," stated Champlin. An elaborate and successful surveillance system was installed at the Paramus store that targeted shoplifters and employee pilferage. A&S initiated a new internal slogan: "Shortage leaves everybody short." Employees were continually updated on shoplifting, internal dishonesty and paperwork problems.

As the decade came to a close, Abraham & Straus, once the most profitable division at Federated Department Stores, became its least profitable. Sales declines, inventory shortages and an ill-conceived merchandise upgrade contributed to A&S's woes. Mel Wilmore, vice-president of stores, stated, "We were going too upscale, too fast. [One executive] wanted to turn A&S into Burdines [a Miami-based Federated division]. It was not who we were. He wanted us to be more upscale. He had the opinion that we were a low class store." Retail consultant John D. Rich told the *New York Times*, "A&S, which had a century of fine image…A&S didn't want to meet the needs of the population in Brooklyn and Long Island, which became lower in income, as middle class residents left."[102]

After it reanalyzed A&S's missteps, a Federated Department Stores *Annual Report* detailed a new traditional strategy for A&S:

> *Brooklyn is New York, too, but as different from Manhattan as though separated by hundreds of miles rather than just the East River. This is the stronghold of Abraham & Straus, which has the largest department store in Federated. Brooklyn itself has an almost totally different socio-economic makeup than it had only a decade ago. Nevertheless, Abraham & Straus, in the heart of Brooklyn, has demonstrated a remarkable capacity to shift with*

the tides of change and has retained and strengthened its leadership position in the community. Despite the nature of its downtown environment, with all of the attendant changes in life-styles, it has remained the pacesetter in its response to the extremely diverse needs of its customer base.

Its third branch store in New Jersey, A&S Monmouth Mall, opened on April 24, 1978. For the first time, Abraham & Straus competed directly in the same shopping complex with Bamberger's, New Jersey's strongest department store company and owned by R.H. Macy. The three-story, 278,000-square-foot A&S was the fifth anchor at the popular Monmouth County shopping complex. A&S claimed that its open-air interior at Monmouth facilitated shopping ease and sightlines. "Courteous service is a long-standing tradition," advertised A&S, setting it apart from competitors, especially Bamberger's.[103]

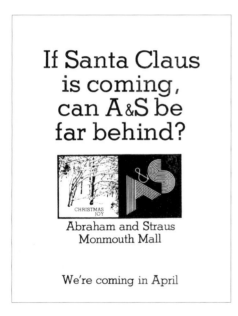

Left: A&S assured Christmas 1977 shoppers that its new Monmouth Mall location would open in the coming months. The Monmouth A&S debuted on April 23, 1978, and joined Bamberger's, Hahne's, Alexander's and JCPenney at the popular Jersey shore shopping center.

Right: A variety of nametags and badges feature the company's familiar, stylized black-and-white A&S logo.

The Monmouth Mall siphoned off business from nearby Seaview Square Mall, home to Stern's and Steinbach, an Asbury Park–based Jersey Shore department store. "Stern's was almost non-existent. You didn't look at them as competition and Steinbach was not a factor to the stores [at Monmouth Mall]," recalled Mel Wilmore. A&S Monmouth met with modest success. "[A&S] would have been better served if we stuck with our stronger markets," added Wilmore.

At the company headquarters, Abraham & Straus stood by its commitment to its downtown Brooklyn location. Throughout the 1970s, A&S Fulton Street weathered the many social and economic challenges that confronted the business. The situation was different at Martin's, Brooklyn's large carriage trade specialty store. Martin's closed its Fulton Street store in May 1979. "There [aren't] enough people coming to the area to buy the kind of merchandise that Martin's carries," stated the company's then-senior vice-president, Murray Apfelbaum.[104] Martin's attempted to stock its downtown location with lower-priced goods, but the experiment alienated its dwindling loyal customer base.

Fulton Street experienced a second loss in October 1980 when the once successful Korvettes chain announced its company-wide closure. A victim of ownership changes and poor merchandising decisions, Korvettes' management shifted the company's focus from hard goods to clothing and experienced disastrous results. Fulton Street champions feared that A&S's closure was imminent. Abraham & Straus corporate officials assured customers that it had no intention of closing the Brooklyn flagship and promised a return to a moderate-to-better merchandise mix. "A&S owned Brooklyn and Long Island," said Mel Whitmore. "The [Brooklyn] customer was a real melting pot; black, white, Jewish. The store itself was growing, but at a slow pace."

CHAPTER 11

Expand and Contract

Abraham & Straus was an exciting store, a "rough and tumble" kind of store.
You never knew what was going to happen next.
—*Mel Wilmore, former group vice-president of stores*

B y the late 1970s, A&S management was often criticized by retail analysts for its "string of poor earnings [which] were the result of the company's inability to sense the public's changing taste and price preferences." Rising operating expenses at its downtown Brooklyn and Hempstead stores added to the company's challenges. However, Federated Department Stores presented an optimistic outlook at A&S. A 1980 Federated Department Stores *Annual Report* praised increased sales performances at the Brooklyn, Manhasset, Woodbridge, Paramus and Queens Center locations: "The key to [A&S's] future progress is a drive to increase sales by refocusing on the traditional Abraham and Straus customer and broadening its base of business."

The monthly company magazine, *Spotlight*, highlighted each of the individual branches over the course of several issues. An article on the Queens Center A&S discussed the "pulse of the store" and "the steady beat of business that says everything is fast and intense [at Queens]." *Spotlight* reported that the Queens Center A&S store was the most important drawing card at that mall, without question. Queens Center was honored for being the largest-volume Abraham & Straus store in the entire chain, aside from the Brooklyn flagship. An article on the Hempstead store hailed improvements in lighting, a new roof and newly relocated departments. *Spotlight* reported that the 1952 Hempstead store benefited from many "long standing, dedicated, and knowledgeable associates" and noted that the recent building updates improved morale among Hempstead's associates. The management at A&S Huntington proudly reported that its store consistently outperformed the mall's Macy's location. *Spotlight* praised Huntington's involvement with many of the area's arts and civic organizations. Executives at Manhasset emphasized "extreme customer service…because that's the way she's [the customer] been brought up." The Manhasset feature stated that many of its customers were extremely loyal and had shopped at the store since its 1965 opening, concluding with, "you never lose an A&S customer, they just change with you." The Monmouth A&S reported that New Jersey customers enjoyed the store's high level of customer service, while the Woodbridge store's Garden Room restaurant and lounge became popular meeting destinations for local clubs and social organizations. *Spotlight* reported that the success at the Garden City store was the result of high standards of service and merchandise. Garden City was "known for the generous amount of time sales associates would spend with a customer, and the courteous attention they give to the customer's needs." The Garden City store "satisfied weekday budget-conscious working people and fashion oriented families who lived in the area and shopped on the weekend." In 1979, Garden City led the entire A&S chain in the percentage of annual sales gains. The Carle Place home store boasted that a new audio department, selections of Early American upholstered furniture and "Maytag Madness" sales led to substantial volume increases.

In February 1980, Federated Department Stores appointed Lasker Meyer as chairman and CEO of Abraham & Straus. Born in Texas, Meyer was an executive at Foley's, a Federated Division based in Houston. Federated officials felt that Meyer's straightforward business approach would help redefine A&S's image and stop "10 years of musical chairs" in the company's executive leadership. "My job was to get expenses to go down and reduce selling space," recalled Meyer. "[Past leadership] tried to make it Bloomingdale's but I went back to the traditional customer—'middle-of-the-road.' [The Brooklyn flagship] was very expensive to operate and just wasn't designed right. It wasn't exciting." Meyer analyzed the Hempstead store and ultimately decided not to mark it for closure. "[Hempstead] was a big building that took up a lot of merchandise. It was awkward for the customer." Meyer also wondered if the small Garden City location warranted elimination. "It was OK, not great," he said.

The Fulton Street store was widely known for its signature elevator court, a central focal point of the store's main floor.

This photograph shows a general view of the Brooklyn store's main floor in February 1993. The elevator court is seen on the right side of the image.

When Mel Wilmore became manager of the Brooklyn store, he found that department managers and sales personnel concentrated primarily on customer service and appropriate merchandise selection. Wilmore wanted to refocus on the store's operation. "I realized that A&S wasn't terribly organized in terms of how they ran their stores." After several months of adjustment, the sales performance at the Brooklyn store improved. When he was promoted to senior vice-president of stores, Wilmore assessed the Hempstead store's numerous problems. "At Hempstead, the neighborhood changed dramatically [in the 1970s]. When the neighborhood changed, the buying went to 'hell in a hand basket.' It became a lower-income African American neighborhood and it changed the whole face of the business [at the Hempstead store]." In the early 1980s, Hempstead reported annual sales of $75 million, but Wilmore stated that "even though we aggressively promoted the store, the transactions [at Hempstead] became much lower [in price]."

When Curtis Champlin served as director of stores, he found similar challenges at the longtime branch. "Hempstead was an old store and there were some very nice customers. The Mayor of Hempstead had me on the

The White Plains A&S was the first of several new stores in the early 1980s. As its first Westchester County location, A&S White Plains anchored the city downtown Galleria shopping complex.

The Mall at Short Hills provided Abraham & Straus an upscale clientele at the New Jersey shopping center. A&S Short Hills joined Bloomingdale's, Bonwit Teller and B. Altman in March 1981.

radio and I talked about the physical appearance of the town. I said that after you drove through Garden City, you'd get to Hempstead and the street signs looked old and the lines in the road had worn away. I told the mayor that Hempstead needed to clean itself up and he was not happy." Champlin also remembered sales declines and physical deterioration at the Babylon store. "I'd visit Babylon about twice a month and I'd see dust on the clothes because they just hadn't moved. The store was falling apart." After a successful redesign of the Juniors' department in Brooklyn, Champlin received a call from Mickey Drexler, vice-president of merchandising. Drexler praised the update. "I thanked Mickey and asked if he could bring some buyers out to

Babylon. I wanted Mickey to have buyers go through the [Babylon] store and fill in merchandise. Buyers travelled to Babylon and wrote orders then and there. We ended up selling things that we used to wait months for. The salespeople [at Babylon] were so excited to be busy. Many of them hadn't walked [to assist customers] in years!"

Abraham & Straus explored other opportunities and expanded into new markets, often with mixed results. On August 6, 1980, A&S opened a new store in downtown White Plains, its first location in Westchester County. Many popular New York stores such as Saks Fifth Avenue, Lord & Taylor, B. Altman and Bloomingdale's had already established Westchester County branches. The new White Plains A&S was part of a new downtown shopping mall named the Galleria.

Abraham & Straus was confident that its full line of merchandise would set it apart from the competition, but the White Plains site never performed up to expectations. "White Plains was a hard one to merchandize," said Curtis Champlin. "It was too big and the competition was fierce. There were stores all over the place [in White Plains] and the [A&S buying staff] never supported it. It didn't do well from the get-go." Although it was not a top performer within the chain, Abraham & Straus never gave up on its White Plains store.

In March 1981, A&S opened a location at the upscale Mall at Short Hills, near Millburn, New Jersey. Anchored by B. Altman, Bonwit Teller and Bloomingdale's, the Mall at Short Hills had originally opened in 1961. A&S at Short Hills was part of a major mall expansion and afforded A&S an opportunity to attract middle- to upper-income shoppers. "At Short Hills, our goal was to be better than Bloomingdales," recalled former store manager William Laupus. "Bonwit Teller was a fashion leader. B. Altman didn't seem to have any particular strength or focus. The mall's new addition wasn't even completed when we opened. I thought that there would be a tremendous problem staffing the store. But we were able to make ties with the community and we got fantastic results. We had great Associates; we strived to be the best and we wanted to be the best. We were very determined when we designed Short Hills. We never compromised and we worked tirelessly and endlessly," said Laupus.

On August 6, 1981, Abraham & Straus entered the crowded and competitive Philadelphia market and anchored the new Court at King of Prussia, in suburban Valley Forge. Philadelphia was an extremely competitive market, and John Wanamaker, Gimbels, Bamberger's and local favorite Strawbridge & Clothier dominated the retail scene. In addition, Lord &

This image depicts the new King of Prussia store, the company's first Philadelphia-area location. It was initially planned to be the first of several stores in the immediate area.

What do you give a city that has everything?

The Liberty Bell. The World Series champs. Ben Franklin. And Riccardo Muti. Face it, Philadelphia, you're one tough city to please. A little cocky. A little smug. And *very* competitive. Kind of like our hometown, Brooklyn, New York.

About a century ago, when the paint was still wet on the Brooklyn Bridge, Abraham and Straus was already answering the question of what to give a city that has everything. New York already had tradition. So we gave it innovation. The first numbered charge accounts. The first horseless delivery carriages. The first "subway store." And cold storage for furs. And multilingual staff. Just to name a few.

New York already had style. So we gave it variety. Whole fashion collections. Floors of home furnishings. Enough new

clothes and furniture to fill the streets and houses of Fifth Avenue . . . or Brooklyn Heights.

New York already had bargains. So we gave it value. And New York already had service. So we gave it the personal touch. Including a remarkable return policy perhaps without equal anywhere.

New York really thought it had everything. Until we showed them what they were missing. And in the process, grew to one of the largest stores in the city, with branches in twelve of New York's and New Jersey's nicest suburbs.

Now Abraham and Straus is coming to one of your nicest suburbs. To The Court at King of Prussia. With the kind of store New Yorkers swear by. What kind of a store will it be? Every bit as exceptional as its thirteen

sister stores in New York and New Jersey. Like every Abraham and Straus store, this one will be filled with innovative new fashions for the whole family and intriguing design concepts for the home.

Like every Abraham and Straus store, this one will offer a depth of merchandise and breadth of price ranges to make shopping a pleasure again.

And like every Abraham and Straus store, this one will continue a tradition of special . . . and community involvement that has been our hallmark for 116 years.

Knowing that you're tough to please, Philadelphia, just makes us feel that much more at home. Already.

Because after all, we're from Brooklyn. And when you come from Brooklyn, you've got to be good.

Abraham and Straus

Opening this Thursday in The Court at King of Prussia.

On August 6, 1981, A&S opened its new store at the Court at King of Prussia. After five years, A&S retrenched from the Philadelphia area.

Taylor, B. Altman, Bonwit Teller and Saks Fifth Avenue operated branch locations within an easy drive of the new center.

King of Prussia was the first of two Abraham & Straus stores planned for the Philadelphia market. The new upscale Court at King of Prussia was adjacent to the existing King of Prussia Plaza. The plaza opened in 1964 and was anchored by John Wanamaker, JCPenney and Gimbels. Over the next two decades, the popular center was frequently updated and modernized. Designed to be the upscale counterpart to the more utilitarian plaza, the new Court at King of Prussia was anchored by Abraham & Straus, Bamberger's and Bloomingdale's. This was the first instance of Abraham & Straus and Bloomingdale's, its upscale Federated sister division, directly competing in the same shopping complex.

Abraham & Straus had little to no familiarity with Philadelphians and struggled to gain an identity. "Philadelphia was our first remote expansion and it was a big mistake," recalled former chairman Lasker Meyer. "It was planned before I arrived [at A&S] and I told people that I didn't think we should do it, but the department managers were so enthusiastic." Former manager Mary Jane Solino agreed. "You can't take a name like Abraham & Straus and put it in a premium mall against stores like Strawbridge's. You're a foreigner. We were unknown, unrecognized. Nobody wanted to know us." Mel Wilmore, vice-president of stores, elaborated, "In all seriousness, people [in Philadelphia] thought we were a law firm." King of Prussia store manager Marc Kravetz told the *Philadelphia Inquirer*, "Our premise is service and quality goods at reasonable prices. We're not in competition with Bloomingdale's. We don't want to be. High-fashion trendy merchandise we're not going to have. That's Bloomingdale's specialty, and they're excellent at it."[105]

On opening day, Carol Channing cut a diamond-studded ribbon as visitors entered a sweepstakes for *Hello, Dolly!* tickets at the Valley Forge Music Fair's "Abraham and Straus Night" and an $1,800 diamond pendant. Soon after "the store New Yorkers swear by" opened its doors, sales at A&S King of Prussia subsided and fell below expectations. "We immediately knew that the store was going to be a problem," said Wilmore.

Even though A&S King of Prussia struggled to gain its retail footing, the company moved forward with its second planned Philadelphia location, at the Willow Grove Park Mall. Willow Grove Park was developed through a partnership between Federated Department Stores and the Rubin Organization. On October 16, 1982, Abraham & Straus joined Bloomingdale's and B. Altman two months after the mall's grand opening.

Get ready to celebrate Opening Day with this instant make-your-own confetti kit. There'll be prizes, surprises, fun for everybody! Bring your confetti & join the parade to A&S Willow Grove Park. The Biggest Marching Band you've ever seen gets off to a terrific Sousa-phonic start at 9 A.M. Follow the band to our ribbon-cutting ceremony at 10 A.M. with John Phillip Sousa III as our special guest. Come early, stay late, bring the kids. It's going to be a terrific day!

The second Philadelphia-area A&S opened on October 16, 1982, at Willow Grove Park. After the opening of Willow Grove, A&S decided to halt all further Philadelphia expansion plans due to sluggish sales and tough competition.

Built on the site of a former popular amusement park, Abraham & Straus presented John Philip Sousa III, grandson of the composer and bandmaster, for its gala celebration. The "Sousa-phonic" event featured the "biggest brassiest marching band you've ever seen." The Willow Grove A&S performed slightly better than its counterpart at King of Prussia.

Abraham & Straus officials soon realized that Philadelphia-area shoppers were very value oriented. "The [Philadelphia] customer is quick to take advantage of A&S promotions," stated Willow Grove manager Marc Kravetz. "So Willow Grove and King of Prussia extend most One Day Sales to Three Day Sales."[106] After the Willow Grove opening, Abraham & Straus halted all further expansion plans into the Philadelphia-area market, which included possible sites in Cherry Hill and Christiana, Delaware.

In 1982, after nine years of sales declines, Abraham & Straus seized on an opportunity to relocate its aging Babylon store. A&S acquired the lease of a recently closed Korvettes store at Massapequa's Sunrise Mall, located only five miles from Babylon. Even though the former Sunrise Mall Korvettes was only half the size of A&S Babylon, the popular enclosed mall afforded an updated shopping environment for its loyal Babylon customers.

A&S needed to remain competitive in the local Massapequa area, and the relocation from Babylon to Sunrise became essential. However, the move was tinged with sadness and nostalgia by associates and customers. Abraham & Straus executives and associates often referred to Babylon as the "Country Club Store" because of its waterfront location; Babylon associates were fondly known as "clamdiggers."[107] Curtis Champlin helped design the new Sunrise Mall store. "Sunrise was just a fraction of the size of Babylon. It did business and was so much fun. I had the privilege of laying it out. I put stockrooms in the center of the store. It better utilized the space." In early 1982, Babylon associates held parties that celebrated the store's history.

Come on Over to A&S Brooklyn

SAY

"HAPPY BIRTHDAY" TO OUR BRIDGE

MAY 1 THROUGH MAY 29

Your guide to shows, exhibits, music, dance, contests, fun and excitement on every floor.

Abraham & Straus and the Brooklyn Bridge played important roles in the borough's history. A&S held a month-long celebration in May 1983 that honored the bridge's 100th birthday.

The *Spotlight* employee magazine referred to the wind down of the Babylon store as the "Sunset Program." From March 4 to March 17, Babylon employees physically moved all necessary paperwork, machines and fixtures to its new Sunrise store; unpacked merchandise; and prepared for the grand opening. No Babylon associates were eliminated as part of the store's Sunrise relocation. On March 18, 1982, store manager Vinny Parlato opened the doors at the new Sunrise Mall Abraham & Straus. Area native and store associate Scott Snyder was not pleased with the store's relocation. "[A&S's] Sunrise was such a let down. It was smaller and there was just so much stuff on the floor. There was just nothing charming about the whole mall."

In 1983, Abraham & Straus refocused company attention on its Brooklyn flagship as part of a major borough event. On May 24, 1983, the Brooklyn Bridge, "the eighth wonder of the world," celebrated its 100th birthday. Abraham & Straus helped lead a month-long anniversary tribute to the iconic structure. The celebration included a flotilla of sailboats in the East River sponsored by A&S. In a procession led by executives from Abraham & Straus and Federated Department Stores, celebrities and dignitaries boarded boats and joined the parade. "Everybody [at A&S] was in great spirits that day," said Curtis Champlin. "Jackie Kennedy and Mrs. Douglas McArthur were on a yacht and tried to pass us [in the flotilla]. The CEO of Federated was furiously jumping up and down since we were paying for the celebration! The Coast Guard told their yacht to get back."

In addition to the boat parade, A&S sponsored a twenty-minute sound and light show on the bridge called "The Eighth Wonder." The show ran nightly from late May through October 10. "A most thrilling display of fireworks," sponsored by A&S and Manufacturers Hanover, capped off the festivities on "Rededication Day."[108] The bridge's anniversary was also featured throughout A&S's Fulton Street store. A Brooklyn Bridge Shop, located on the main floor, sold books, T-shirts, buttons, posters and towels, along with laminated pieces of the bridge's original wooden walkway. Brooklyn College, the Brooklyn Children's Museum, the Brooklyn Botanic Garden, the Long Island Historical Society and the Brooklyn Academy of Music sponsored programs held throughout the store's first eight floors. The Calabash Dance Company, Izulu Dance Theatre, Brooklyn Philharmonic and St. Luke's Chamber Ensemble also presented a series of cultural performances. The employee training room, located on the sixth floor, featured daily 12:30 p.m. screenings of the movie *A Tree Grows in Brooklyn*. Daily educational lectures and workshops rounded out the store's Brooklyn Bridge celebration.

In the summer of 1984, the long-awaited $24 million Fulton Mall was finally completed. New trees, renovated storefronts, brick sidewalks and wooden benches brought a sense of pride and optimism to the downtown shopping district. Unfortunately, the area was unable to fill the large

This photograph shows the Fulton Street frontage of the flagship Brooklyn store in the early 1990s.

The Fulton Mall, as seen from the front of Abraham & Straus, appears busy in this 1993 image.

vacancies created by the closing of Martin's and Korvettes. Two years after its completion, Fulton Mall received criticism over its inability to spur future commercial investment. "There is a considerable feeling nowadays that the beautiful elements like new façades and trees are simply decorative, not attractions," stated the publisher of the national newsletter *Downtown Idea Exchange*.[109]

Many Abraham & Straus officials were pleased with the changes. "Fulton Street was dramatically improved and cleaned up. [The merchants] ended up controlling the streets. We had a big push with police to remove people who sold goods out on the streets. A bank moved in which was fabulous and a whole section of the street was brand new," said Curtis Champlin. He recalled one merchant who challenged the aesthetic of the new pedestrian mall. "I had to deal with a guy across from my office who often used a loud speaker. I kept telling him that unless you want to get in trouble, turn that thing down! Every time he tried to use the loud speaker, we sent over our security until he stopped." Between the Fulton Mall project and successful openings at Short Hills and Sunrise, Abraham & Straus enjoyed increased profitability. It was a sign of rebirth for the Brooklyn department store firm, but upcoming changes in the retail industry would threaten its legacy and future.

CHAPTER 12

Remember Me on Herald Square

They surely won't pout,
Nor probably cry.
But maybe they'll shout
And I'm telling you why:
A&S is coming to town.
—Newsday, *editorial, April 28, 1987*

By the middle of the decade, the department store industry was in turmoil. Century-old retailers fell victim to mergers, closures, leveraged buyouts and massive layoffs. Department stores traditionally appealed to a loyal middle-class customer base. As competition for price and selection increased, many middle-class shoppers elected to patronize higher-end specialty stores, independent boutiques or popular discount stores like Caldor, Bradlees and Kmart. When the middle class shrank, traditional department stores became less relevant. Stores engaged in excessive promotions that trained customers to delay purchases until their weekend sale days. Large department store companies struggled with high labor costs and expensive maintenance costs for their aging buildings. Weaker department stores fell victim to takeover and closures. Investors frequently sought out vulnerable retailers for their real estate value rather than their established trade.

The New York Metropolitan Area experienced many department store ownership changes and closures. In 1986, Ohrbach's, an A&S co-anchor at the Smith Haven and Woodbridge malls, announced its liquidation. Its Dutch owner, Breninkmeyer, pulled the plug on the legendary popularly priced apparel store. Ohrbach's served as an important anchor in Manhattan's Thirty-Fourth Street shopping district. In 1987, New York developers Steven Roth and Donald J. Trump purchased large shares of Alexander's stock in an effort to acquire the prominent Upper East Side Alexander's building and land, located on Fifty-Eighth and Lexington Avenue. In order to settle a huge debt owed to Citicorp, Trump was forced to turn over his Alexander's shares, forfeiting any possibility of acquiring the property for his personal use. On May 15, 1992, after years of unprofitable competition with discount houses, Alexander's filed for Chapter 11 bankruptcy protection and began a liquidation sale at all eleven stores. In New Jersey, the Bamberger's name was replaced by Macy's, its parent corporation. In October 1986, loyal Garden State customers lost a large swath of local identity when the Bamberger's name was erased.

In 1986, Associated Dry Goods—the owner of Lord & Taylor, Hahne's, J.W. Robinson's and numerous other store divisions—was acquired by the May Department Stores Company. Hahne's, its New Jersey department store division, decided to move its headquarters from Newark to Paramus's Garden State Plaza. The closing of Hahne's longtime flagship store left a commercial void, along with a large vacant structure, in Newark's central business district. In 1985, the Altman Foundation decided to "increase its assets for philanthropic purposes" and sell its B. Altman & Company department store business.[110] The elegant, large, carriage trade store was sold in 1986 to an investor group. Just one year later, the group sold the B. Altman stores to Austrian developer L.J. Hooker. Hooker had grand nationwide plans for B. Altman but became crippled by debt. Hooker's August 1989 bankruptcy filing lead to B. Altman's liquidation just three months later.

The Philadelphia retail market also fell victim to the industry's changes. In 1986, Philadelphia's iconic John Wanamaker stores were placed on the auction block and acquired by Washington's Woodward & Lothrop. In a grand effort to remain a family-operated business, Strawbridge & Clothier spent large amounts of time and money and successfully fought off a hostile takeover attempt by financier Ronald Baron. After it won the battle for independence, the company decided to strengthen its market position by further investing in Philadelphia's suburbs. On October 29, 1986, Strawbridge & Clothier purchased the two Philadelphia-area Abraham & Straus locations. The company's purchase ended "several years of

A&S quickly moved into the former Gimbels Green Acres Mall store after that company's liquidation in September 1986. *Courtesy of the Scott Snyder Collection.*

disappointment [at the Philadelphia area A&S locations] in which it had a difficult time persuading Philadelphians to shop at its stores."[111] The King of Prussia store closed in early 1987, followed by Willow Grove in January 1988. Both eventually reopened as Strawbridge's.

One of the industry's biggest casualties was Gimbels, a once mighty department store that frequently battled Macy's in promotions and sales. Gimbels' massive Manhattan flagship store, located just one block south of Macy's Herald Square, was immortalized in the movie *Miracle on 34th Street*. As part of its story line, the beloved holiday movie portrayed the fierce rivalry between Macy's and Gimbels. Reluctant suburban expansion, poor management decisions and stagnant merchandise offerings hampered Gimbels' identity and purpose in the crowded New York market. As Abraham & Straus, Macy's and Bloomingdale's updated their businesses and followed consumer tastes, Gimbels stood still. In January 1986, British American Tobacco, Gimbels' owner since 1973, decided that the store would cease operations unless a buyer could be found. In May 1986, Gimbels, unable to sell the business as an ongoing concern, announced that its New York stores—along with its other divisions in Philadelphia, Pittsburgh and Milwaukee—would shut their doors. Gimbels' departure left numerous empty buildings throughout New York's retail districts and area shopping malls.

The shuttering of Gimbels at Valley Stream's Green Acres Mall provided a desirable expansion opportunity for Abraham & Straus. In October 1986, A&S purchased the closed Gimbels Green Acres location and reopened it in a matter of weeks. The new store performed beyond expectations and reversed years of sales declines experienced at the former Gimbels location. Chairman Chaim Edelstein stated, "We took over a Gimbels store [at Green Acres] that did about $30 million [in sales] in its last year. We are already [within two years] exceeding that by 50 percent."[112] However, the Green Acres A&S placed increased sales pressure on the aging A&S Hempstead store, located just seven miles away.

Gimbels' exit afforded another major opportunity for the Brooklyn-based retailer. On April 23, 1987, A&S announced plans for a new 310,000-square-foot department store in the former Gimbels Manhattan building. The new A&S was the department store's first entry into Manhattan and was part of a new vertical shopping mall named "A&S Plaza." The project, designed for one hundred retail shops and 800,000 square feet of office space, was carved

A building model from March 1987 shows the proposed design of the new A&S Plaza, an indoor retail and commercial center carved within the former Gimbels on Manhattan's Thirty-Third Street. *Courtesy of the RTKL Associates Collection.*

Although the main entrances into the A&S Plaza mall were situated on the Avenue of the Americas, direct street access into the A&S store was located on Thirty-Second and Thirty-Third Streets. *Courtesy of the RTKL Associates Collection.*

within the former Gimbels building at Sixth Avenue and Thirty-Third Street. The new A&S marked the first department store built within Manhattan since 1980, when Alexander's opened its World Trade Center branch. The location placed A&S Plaza in direct competition with Macy's flagship store. Abraham & Straus executives believed that the area's pedestrian and subway traffic provided an opportunity for increased customer traffic in the heavily traveled shopping district. A&S senior vice-president Francesco Cantarella told the *New York Daily News*, "If you're a department store in New York, you have to have an outlet in Manhattan to be one of the major players."[113] The new A&S Plaza anticipated a fall 1988 grand opening.

Robert Campeau played a pivotal role in America's changing department store industry. A successful and prominent Canadian real estate developer, Campeau was "drawn to retailing by a vision of linking it to real estate." In October 1986, with the backing of several large banks and investment houses, Campeau aggressively pursued the Allied Stores Corporation, the holding company of Stern's, Jordan Marsh, Maas Brothers and twenty other retail divisions. Campeau was intent on becoming a major American mall developer and felt that the purchase of Allied would help fill anchor spaces in his shopping centers. In early November 1986, the Allied board finally succumbed and sold the company for $3.6 billion. Campeau largely funded the purchase with junk bonds, which resulted in insurmountable debt. In order to manage the financial burden, sixteen of Allied's twenty-four divisions were sold, merged or liquidated. Managerial and executive job losses were staggering.

Campeau, enamored of Bloomingdale's and undaunted by debt, continued his retail-buying streak. With a strong portfolio of retail stores and real estate holdings, Federated became a prime takeover target. In addition to Campeau, Federated received interest from R.H. Macy & Company, the May Department Stores Company and Dillard Department Stores. After an aggressive bidding war, Campeau "captured" Federated on April 1, 1988. His $6.5 billion purchase price added $5 billion to his current debt load. Market analysts questioned the deal, as Campeau's annual interest payments ballooned to an unrealistic $869 million. *Fortune* magazine called Campeau's purchase of Federated "the biggest looniest deal ever." The magazine wondered how a man with a "widely publicized history of emotional breakdowns, volatile behavior, and aggressive business practices convinced some of the country's lending firms to fund his takeover binge?"[114]

At a press conference held soon after the Federated purchase, Campeau addressed skeptics and outlined his future plans for his latest retail acquisition. He enthusiastically discussed a possible countrywide expansion of Bloomingdale's. In response to Abraham & Straus, Campeau briefly commented, "A&S will be streamlined."[115] A&S employees and Brooklyn residents feared that the Fulton Street store would be shuttered and the entire chain eliminated. Campeau had developed a reputation for maximizing store efficiency through job cuts. However, upon his first visit to the Brooklyn headquarters, Robert Campeau was welcomed by A&S employees and executives. "[Campeau] came to Brooklyn, walked into the boardroom, and we all stood up and clapped. He was so excited," remembered Curtis Champlin, vice-president of stores. But in June 1988, 269 Abraham & Straus positions at its Brooklyn headquarters were eliminated, in addition to 525 positions at its suburban branches. Four senior A&S vice-presidents were dismissed, and numerous buying and clerical positions were cut. With a total workforce of 11,000, no sales associates were eliminated at A&S. A company press release stated, "By preserving the present level of sales associates, A&S will continue to provide its customers with a high quality of service."[116]

A&S proceeded with its Manhattan plans despite the company being streamlined. Campeau "welcomed the chance [for A&S] to succeed in

Manhattan."[117] He estimated that the new location would generate $100 million in sales in its first year. In addition to the A&S Plaza project, Campeau initially discussed replacing the aging Fulton Street store with a 6.4-million-square-foot commercial and retail project, but no formal plans were developed. A&S decided to "focus its merchandise mix [in Manhattan] on moderate to upper-moderate clothing," an area that the A&S executives felt its neighboring competitor, Macy's, neglected. Chairman Chaim Edelstein told the *New York Times* that the new Manhattan store "would ignore designer clothing carried in stores like Macy's and Bloomingdale's. There will be no Ralph Lauren clothing, except in the children's department."[118] Douglas A. Schuler, former vice-president of operations, recalled A&S's entry into Manhattan: "This is a highly competitive business and we were now going head to head with Macy's. [A&S] had a dominant presence in the suburbs so we weren't a total stranger [in Manhattan]."

As opening day grew closer, A&S officials scrambled to stock and finish the store. "We ended up having to load the new store up at night or else our trucks would get stuck in traffic," remembered Schuler. "It took a lot of time and effort and [with an eight-story building] velocity was critical." On September 14, 1989, A&S officially opened its new Manhattan store. The

By the 1990s, many display windows had been removed along the Livingston Street frontage.

119

In 1993, a prominent display window at the Livingston and Hoyt Street intersection was covered over with the A&S logo.

A&S Plaza mall featured a 212-foot-high atrium and more than two miles of neon lighting along the building's exterior. The A&S store combined Art Deco details, as a nod to the Brooklyn flagship, with elaborate video displays and jukeboxes. A concierge helped customers obtain theater tickets, dinner reservations and local transportation. Despite a *New York Times* article that referred to the A&S Plaza store as "marginally profitable," Edelstein was "very pleased" with the store's results.[119] "We were next to Macy's, the largest store in the world, and we were doing $100 million in [annual] sales."

Drowning in debt, Campeau's credit line dwindled, and manufacturers halted deliveries to his department stores. Just one day after the A&S Plaza's gala opening, Campeau agreed to a $250 million loan from Olympia & York, a Canadian property development firm. In exchange, Olympia & York gained managerial influence on the boards of Federated and Allied, and Campeau was removed as company chairman. The loan did not ultimately solve financial woes, and crippling debt payments mounted. On January 15, 1990, the Campeau Corporation filed for Chapter 11 bankruptcy protection. A&S chairman Chaim Edelstein, along with President Leonard Marcus, placed full-page newspaper advertisements that notified customers of the bankruptcy filing. Both executives informed customers that all store merchandise, credit and return policies would remain unchanged. "Please rest assured that we are operating as usual. Our stores will remain open the same hours as before and will be staffed with the same knowledgeable and professional sales associates you have come to know and trust." Other Federated and Allied divisions—including Rich's, Burdines, Bloomingdale's and Jordan Marsh—posted similar notices in their local newspapers.

Although it protected company assets and reassured merchandise suppliers, the bankruptcy filing also allowed the company to break lease obligations. By March 1990, the Campeau Corporation considered selling its Hempstead store to raise badly needed funds. Once the nation's largest suburban department store, the Hempstead A&S was in "deplorable condition" and generated sales per square foot far below the national average.[120] Although the store had fallen into disrepair, its real estate was extremely valuable. Chairman Chaim Edelstein insisted, "Even in its twilight, Hempstead was still making money, volume-wise. But it was a freestanding store. That was great in the 1950s and 1960s but it all changed when everybody wanted to go to the malls." In early June 1992, Abraham & Straus management gathered its 240 Hempstead employees around the building's escalator bank and notified staff that the store would soon close. The announcement devastated Hempstead village officials. Community leaders mourned the decision and stated that the store's departure would be a "crushing blow to the community, which has been grappling with economic decline for more than a decade."[121] The store ended its forty-year run on October 8, 1992.

On February 5, 1992, only two years after its initial filing, A&S's parent company, Federated, emerged from bankruptcy protection. During the bankruptcy process, Federated had restructured the corporation by streamlining buying and credit systems and closed unprofitable stores. The reorganized corporation was renamed Federated Department Stores Inc. Creditors forgave approximately $3 billion of Campeau's former $8 billion debt load. As part of the reorganization plan, Campeau's former creditors were issued stock in the new company. Retail analysts stated that it was "the first large department store chain ever to emerge from a Chapter 11 bankruptcy."[122]

On March 6, 1992, Federated made a bold move and announced that its Boston-based Jordan Marsh division would be merged into Abraham & Straus. Deemed as a cost-cutting measure, more than five hundred Jordan Marsh executive, buying and clerical positions were eliminated. Author and historian Anthony Sammarco stated, "Once called New England's Greatest Department Store, Jordan Marsh had been 'the' department store in Boston

In a 1994 *Federated Department Stores' Fact Book*, the company lists all locations of the combined A&S/Jordan Marsh division.

for over a century. It became a treasured part of middle-class life of shoppers." Bostonians were angered that the 140-year-old Boston department store was losing its local authority. Federated officials decided to keep the Jordan Marsh name and not further alienate New England customers. All executive decisions at the Jordan Marsh stores were transferred to the new A&S/Jordan Marsh Brooklyn headquarters. The *Boston Globe* reported:

> *No one questions the mercantile savvy of Abraham & Straus....Jordan Marsh had its Eben Jordan, credited by some with having invented the maxim, "The customer is always right." But A&S had its Abraham Abraham, who backed the Brooklyn Bridge. A&S has survived depressions, world wars and, above all, arch rival Macy's....But in the hyper-competitive New York department store market, Abraham & Straus' philosophy was to allow someone else to be the prognosticator of fashion and then stock more of that fashion in more sizes and colors than anyone else. That echoes Jordan's own merchandising philosophy in New England.*[123]

Former A&S vice-president Douglas Schuler remembered, "The merger with Jordan Marsh was about reducing expenses. It was a little less of an issue from the public's perception. It felt like a big step but it became one of several consolidations [within Federated]." Federated predicted an annual savings of $25 million from the merger. Chairman Chaim Edelstein felt the merger achieved positive results since "A&S and Jordan Marsh ran their businesses very similarly." Although the two cities seemed far apart, Edelstein stated, "these days, Macy's runs all of their stores out of New York." In July 1993, as a result of the consolidation, Jordan Marsh stores in Yorktown Heights, New York, and Trumbull, Connecticut, assumed the A&S nameplate. The two former Jordan Marsh stores were better served under A&S's promotional umbrella. "As a Jordan Marsh, [Trumbull and Yorktown] had to rely on advertising out of Boston," said Edelstein. "They weren't merchandized any differently but they performed much better as A&S."

Backed by a newly reorganized Federated corporation, A&S opened a state-of-the-art store at Long Island's largest shopping mall, Roosevelt Field. On October 17, 1992, A&S celebrated "a rare event in good times and a true anomaly in recent recessionary years" with its new Roosevelt Field branch, housed in a rebuilt former Alexander's store. A&S vice-president Douglas Schuler claimed that "Roosevelt Field became a huge factor" in the division's

The imposing Roosevelt Field A&S was located on the site of a former Alexander's and helped solidify the company's Long Island presence and dominance. *Courtesy of the Scott Snyder Collection.*

On June 27, 1993, the Trumbull, Connecticut and Yorktown Heights, New York Jordan Marsh locations were renamed A&S. Brooklyn management decided that the stores should be called A&S and benefit from the company's New York City media market. Both locations were former Bridgeport-based D.M. Read locations and were acquired by Jordan Marsh in March 1987. When they transitioned to Macy's in 1995, the Trumbull and Yorktown stores had operated under four different nameplates within eight years.

success and helped solidify the company's dominant position on Long Island. Joel Evans, the director of Hofstra University's Retail Management Institute, stated, "This is a milestone for Federated and Roosevelt Field. I think it's exciting for Long Island, too." Some associates had a premonition that regarded A&S's new Roosevelt Field location. Associates felt that A&S purposely designed a very fine store just so it could transition well into a Bloomingdale's.[124] "At Roosevelt Field's grand opening," retail analyst Alan Millstein told *Newsday*, "A&S has a longstanding relationship with Long Island shoppers. There are more carpets in more homes in Levittown from A&S than anyone else....As the Long Island Expressway opened, A&S was right behind."[125]

In February 1992, R.H. Macy & Company, battered by chaotic management and industry changes, filed for bankruptcy protection. A corporate-level leveraged buyout in 1985, designed to protect Macy's from takeover attempts and retain executive talent, had failed to achieve results and saddled the company with unmanageable debt payments. The 1988 purchase of Federated's Bullock's, Bullocks Wilshire and I. Magnin divisions placed additional financial strain on the Macy organization. After the 1992 bankruptcy filing, Macy's closed stores and merged divisions. The company wanted to remain an independent department store organization, but "its weakened state and several strategic mishaps doomed it to become just another takeover target."

In July 1994, R.H. Macy & Company agreed to be acquired by Federated Department Stores for $4.1 billion. The merger united 450 Federated and Macy stores in thirty-five states and estimated total annual sales of $14 billion. Upon the merger's announcement, the *Wall Street Journal* reported, "Federated is expected to expand on, not reduce, the Macy's name. Federated

A recent modernization and renovation shows the second-floor elevator lobby in 1993.

By the early 1990s, the Brooklyn store's fourth-floor Garden Room restaurant had been simply renamed the A&S Restaurant.

The windows of the Brooklyn restaurant were eventually covered over with plastic panels that portrayed colorful plants and flowers.

won't comment, but industry observers expect some of its Abraham & Straus stores to be converted to Macy's locations."[126] The *New York Times* firmly noted, "Macy's and Abraham & Straus are so competitive that they make it hard for each other to make any money in the New York City area, so they are likely to be consolidated in a merger."[127]

Operating functions of Macy's New York, A&S and Jordan Marsh were slowly consolidated into a new division called Macy's East. Although its future as a retail division was in doubt, A&S's Brooklyn headquarters proceeded with its new Nanuet Mall location, then under construction. The 180,000-square-foot Nanuet helped anchor a twenty-one-store expansion at the Rockland County mall. As part of the center's development A&S Nanuet opened on November 12, 1994. The Nanuet opening included an appearance by soap opera star Michael E. Knight. The *Journal News* reported, "The line for Knight's autograph [at A&S] was so long that it literally extended out of the door and out onto the second story of the parking deck."[128] Within two months, the brand-new Nanuet Mall A&S, along with the entire Abraham & Straus division, was renamed.

On January 8, 1995, Federated announced the dissolution of the A&S/ Jordan Marsh division. More than 650 A&S/Jordan Marsh corporate-level positions, from merchandise managers to buyers, advertising personnel and

An advertisement in the *Journal News* announced the November 1994 opening of the Nanuet Mall A&S. The entire A&S division announced its dissolution only two months later.

photographers, were eliminated. Most of the A&S/Jordan Marsh divisions were folded into Federated's Macy's East or Stern's divisions. The consolidation ultimately removed the Abraham & Straus name, a longtime piece of the borough's history and identity, from the Brooklyn landscape. On April 30, 1995, Abraham & Straus locations in Brooklyn, Huntington, Manhasset, Valley Stream, Yorktown, Carle Place, Paramus, Short Hills and Trumbull were renamed Macy's. Former locations in Lake Grove, Massapequa, Monmouth, White Plains and the recently opened store at the Nanuet Mall were transferred to Stern's, Federated's moderately priced division. The opulent three-year-old Roosevelt Field store became Bloomingdale's and replaced that division's Garden City location.

Some A&S Nanuet Mall customers were incensed that the two-month-old location would be transitioned to Stern's. "Why did they bother to open it if they were going to close is so soon?" asked one New City resident. "I love A&S and I would go to New Jersey to shop there. Then they finally opened one here. This is all like a big tease."[129] Manhattan's A&S Plaza store became the subject of controversy among the mall's tenants. "Stern's may not be sexy, but experts say sexy is not what [Manhattan's] retail landscape needs," reported a *Crain's New York Business* report.[130] Tenants reluctantly accepted A&S's transition to Stern's as opposed to a vacant storefront. The Garden City A&S, the company's first and smallest branch, remained in operation until May 28, 1995. In its final years, the Garden City store had been relegated to more of a clearinghouse than a retail store. Although it was small in size, A&S was always reluctant to close its Garden City location. "We figured that it wasn't worth the bad feelings if we pulled out [years ago]. It ultimately wasn't a drain on the company," remembered Vice-President Curtis Champlin.

In a message to its customers, Abraham & Straus published a full-page newspaper advertisement that discussed the merger and the future of the store locations. "We've shared so much over the past 130 years. We've

The Manhasset store, located on the north shore's famous Miracle Mile, was one of the company's best-performing locations. *Courtesy of the Scott Snyder Collection.*

The Walt Whitman Mall A&S continually expanded over the years. After Federated merged A&S into Macy's in 1995, Walt Whitman became the first mall in the country that housed two Macy's locations in the same center. That particular arrangement was short-lived. *Courtesy of the Scott Snyder Collection.*

This photograph shows the A&S Garden City store in its final years. The location became a clearance center after Roosevelt Field opened. Garden City closed on May 28, 1995, and was the final store to operate under the A&S nameplate. *Courtesy of the Scott Snyder Collection.*

The downtown Brooklyn A&S prepares for its changeover to Macy's in April 1995.

weathered hundreds of changes together, celebrated holidays together, followed each other to the suburbs. We've opened new stores, even opened the Brooklyn Bridge together....[The consolidation of A&S into Macy's] ensures that the retailing landscape of the tri-state area will continue to be the most exciting—and most competitive—in the country....The coming months will be exciting ones for us. And for you. The future looks bright... we invite you to share it with us."

Prior to the 1995 merger announcement, Abraham & Straus had eliminated departments and floor space at its flagship Fulton Street store. For some longtime Brooklynites, Abraham & Straus, once the country's third-largest department store building, had lost its cache over the years. New York City councilman Alan N. Maisel, the representative of Brooklyn's Forty-Sixth District, was a former employee at the Fulton Street Abraham & Straus store: "My mother loved Abraham & Straus because she was able to buy good quality products there. I thought it was a better store than Macy's. I was sorry to see the name go but I understood the business decision. I had been in the [Fulton Street] store [at the time of the merger announcement] and there was no point in going back. It wasn't A&S. It wasn't that unique anymore. You could just go to any Macy's."

CHAPTER 13

Wrap Desk

One by one, they disappeared. The glittering Paramount, Albee and Fox movie palaces; Ebbets Field and the resident, sometimes champion, Dodgers; the flagship Abraham & Straus store; the exciting Steeplechase in Coney Island.
—New York Daily News, *February 21, 1999*

When Federated consolidated Abraham & Straus into its Manhattan-based Macy's East division, the company celebrated with a number of special events at the Fulton Street store. A series of twenty-four nostalgic window displays, located along the Livingston Street frontage, chronicled the history of Brooklyn and the store's 125-year relationship with the borough. Cartoon character visits, children's activities and Thanksgiving Parade balloons rounded out the opening festivities. Macy's pledged $100 million in renovations to the former Abraham & Straus stores. Many Fulton Street shoppers welcomed Macy's into Brooklyn. A number of area residents openly complained that the Fulton Street store appeared "distressed," "run-down," "grim" and "neglected" and desperately needed a full renovation.

In 1995, six former Abraham & Straus locations were absorbed into Stern's division. By 2000, Federated had grown frustrated with Stern's as it struggled to maintain sufficient market share and show adequate growth potential. Federated announced in September 2000 that it was pulling the plug on the former Manhattan A&S Plaza and Nanuet Mall Stern's stores. Federated reported that sales figures had plummeted after the Manhattan

The exterior Art Deco–inspired entrance to the Manhattan A&S Plaza store was located on the side of the former Gimbels store. Opened in 1989, the A&S Plaza store transitioned to a Stern's against the wishes of the plaza's tenants. *Courtesy of the Scott Snyder Collection.*

The Manhattan A&S Plaza store was converted to the Stern's format in May 1995. The midtown shopping complex was renamed the Manhattan Mall. Stern's left the Manhattan Mall in 2001.

store transitioned from A&S to Stern's. "Stern's [in Manhattan] did little to promote itself," the *New York Times* reported. "The store seemed a bit fuddy-duddy…a bit long in the tooth."[131] Federated stated that the Nanuet Mall Stern's, a former A&S store, was too large to operate profitably. Nanuet Mall was also threatened by the new large Palisades Center, located only four miles away. In February 2001, Federated axed the entire Stern's division. Former A&S locations in Smith Haven, Sunrise, Valley Stream and Monmouth were soon closed, and others were converted into additional Macy's locations.

In July 2005, a *New York Times* article praised the Fulton Street building's architectural contributions but criticized the appearance of its neighborhood. "Fulton Street has fallen far below the original aspirations of the 1880s, and now has raucously cheap, off-price stores. So Macy's, which took over Abraham & Straus operations…sets a high tone for the area, and its retail frontage is dignity incarnate in the midway of flashy chrome, bright plastic, and comparable materials."[132] But as time wore on, Macy's physical condition of its downtown Brooklyn store deteriorated. Federated addressed the store's decline by closing off departments and shrinking the store's massive square footage. In August 2015, Macy's chairman and CEO Terry Lundgren

After Federated's 1994 purchase of Macy's, A&S closed its Woodbridge, New Jersey store and sold its lease to Sears.

The Monmouth Mall A&S became a Stern's store in May 1995. Stern's promised big changes and sales opportunities for the former A&S customers. Stern's closed the store in 2001.

released a statement: "In recent years, it has become clear that our Fulton Street store requires major improvements in order to serve the Brooklyn of today, as well as future generations of customers....The aim is to create a store that fuses Macy's traditions with Brooklyn's local flavor to create a modern environment of cutting-edge style and hip, urban attitude."[133]

In January 2016, as downtown Brooklyn experienced a commercial and retail rebirth, Macy's sold its Fulton Street location to Tishman Speyer, one of the city's largest and oldest commercial developers, for $270 million. Under the terms of sale, Macy's agreed to occupy just the first four floors and basement and complete a full renovation. Tishman Speyer planned a 620,000-square-foot creative office hub on the building's upper floors, along with a ten-story glass structure. The complex helped address Brooklyn's shortage of world-class office space. Designed in collaboration with Perkins Eastman and the Shimoda Group, the $500 million project was named the Wheeler, a historical nod to its original 1873 construction. A 2019 completion date is anticipated.

Although its name vanished in 1995, many New Yorkers still fondly recall Abraham & Straus. Former A&S chairman Chaim Y. Edelstein remembered

Above: The Fulton Street Macy's frontage awaits renovation in this 2017 image.

Left: Signs posted throughout the downtown Brooklyn Macy's in 2017 promise a major redesign of the store.

An aerial view of the store's main floor prior to the store's recent renovation. Historical photographs of the store, dating back to the Wechsler & Abraham days, still adorn the walls.

The main floor of the downtown Brooklyn Macy's shows some of the Art Deco decorative columns before the store's major renovation.

This 2016 photograph shows the Fulton Street frontage of the downtown Macy's. The upper floors of the original 1873 building had been repainted green.

By 2016, the main floor at the Brooklyn store was engulfed in construction. The elevator court had been closed, and sections of the street floor were curtained off.

A&S as "one of the best downtown stores in the world." Edelstein said, "We were not Bloomingdale's but we were a very value-oriented fashion store. [A&S] competed against Bamberger's and Macy's and I think we did a pretty good job. Macy's was completely different from us. We were much stronger in terms of fashion and people felt a lot of loyalty to our company." Scott Snyder, a former A&S associate and inventory control employee, stated that his mother lived within walking distance of the Fulton Street store. He remembered the building's charm and the company's commitment to community programs. "There was a lot of love for A&S's," said Snyder. "They just had a certain culture that the other stores didn't have. When [former Brooklynites] moved to the outer boroughs, they stayed with A&S's. They were just so familiar with it." Snyder still comes in contact with present and former New Yorkers and finds that people "just light up" with a mere mention of A&S.

Downtown Brooklyn's current redevelopment, including a facelift of Abraham & Straus's former flagship store, inspires hope. Despite some of the building's original architectural accoutrements being lost in the renovation, it is heartening that in 2017, unlike most American cities, Brooklyn still houses a downtown department store. Former borough

An artist rendition shows a newly designed main floor at the downtown Brooklyn Macy's.

According to this rendition, the main entrance to the department store will shift over to the original 1873 building.

president Marty Markowitz has a reflective yet optimistic outlook on downtown Brooklyn. Markowitz fondly recalled Abraham & Straus and its economic and cultural legacy but acknowledged that the company's struggles were symptomatic of the entire department store industry's challenges: "The demise of A&S reflected a lot of what was happening in Brooklyn and was certainly a reflection of urban America."

A champion of Brooklyn, Markowitz stated, "Although we will always miss Abraham & Straus, I am happy to tell you that Brooklyn is now home to some of the greatest retailers in the country. Mom & Pop stores still exist side-by-side with the big national chains. Brooklyn is going through an unbelievable rejuvenification and renaissance and is in many ways stronger than it was back in the fifties, and certainly the sixties. [Brooklyn's] come around, that's for sure. We can't go back to yesterday but there's every chance that tomorrow is going to be even better. I'm confident of it."

The Great Abraham & Straus Cheesecake Contest

I n the late 1960s, the Great Abraham & Straus Cheesecake Contest was inaugurated. Every March, hundreds of amateur bakers descended on the Brooklyn store, along with most A&S branches. A team of judges reviewed the cakes and tasted a sliver of each submission. After a list of finalists was compiled, contestants gathered at the Brooklyn store for further deliberation. Each amateur baker was required to bake his or her cake in the Brooklyn store kitchen. A team of four to five New York City chefs selected the winning cheesecakes. Monetary prizes were awarded to the top three prizewinners. The Great Abraham & Straus Cheesecake Contest became a popular and beloved tradition.

"It's all a plan to involve customers in things that give them pleasure," stated Mrs. Gilds Block, A&S vice-president of sales promotion. "Of course, we hope that afterwards as they wander through the store, they will think 'isn't A&S a nice place to be.'" Today, winning cheesecake recipes can be found in local newspapers such as *Newsday* and the *New York Times*, on websites and personal recipe cards. The recipes posted here include the recipe of the department store's signature cheesecake, along with other prizewinners from the contest's two-decade run. Every attempt was made to identify each recipe's creator.

A&S Cheesecake

6 ounces soft, creamy farmer cheese
1 pound, 14 ounces cream cheese, at room temperature (30 ounces total)
1 cup sugar
3 eggs plus 2 yolks, at room temperature
2 teaspoons fresh lemon juice
1 ½ teaspoons vanilla extract
¾ cup sour cream
¾ cup heavy cream

Place a rack in the upper third of the oven and preheat oven to 350 degrees. Spray a 9-inch springform pan with non-stick cooking spray and line the bottom with a round of parchment paper. Spray the parchment. Wrap the outside of the pan with aluminum foil to prevent any water from coming in from the water bath.

Press the farmer cheese through a fine mesh strainer to ensure that the curds are fine. In the bowl of a stand mixer fitted with the paddle attachment (or use a large bowl and a hand mixer), mix the farmer cheese, cream cheese and sugar. Beat on low speed for two minutes, or until smooth, scraping down the side of the bowl.

Add the eggs and egg yolks, one at a time, scraping down the bowl and paddle or beaters after each addition. Beat in the lemon juice and vanilla. Scrape down the bowl and paddle. Still on low speed, beat in the sour cream. Slowly add the heavy cream, beating until blended; stop to scrape down the bowl and paddle every 30 seconds. Gently press the finished batter through a fine mesh strainer.

Pour the mixture into the prepared pan, scraping every last bit out of the bowl with a rubber spatula. Place the pan in a larger baking or a roasting pan and place on the oven rack. Pour enough hot water into the baking pan to come halfway up the side of the springform pan. Bake 1 hour.

Turn off the oven; do not open the oven door. Leave in the oven another 45 minutes to 1 hour; the cake will be golden and set (if you don't have a window, open the oven door quickly to check).

Remove the cake from the oven, remove from the water bath to a rack and cool about 2 hours until it reaches room temperature. Refrigerate at least 4 hours.

To serve, run a knife around the inside of the side of the springform pan and remove the side. Allow the cake to stand at room temperature 20 minutes before serving. Makes 16 services.

Grandma's Cheesecake
Denise Nowak, Ridgewood, Queens, First Prize, 1988 (courtesy Newsday*)*

1 cup graham cracker crumbs
2 teaspoons butter, softened
2 teaspoons sugar
32 ounces cream cheese, softened
2 cups granulated sugar
6 eggs
2 pints sour cream
2 teaspoons vanilla extract

Mix together graham cracker crumbs, butter and sugar. Press into bottom of a buttered 10-inch springform pan. Combine cream cheese and sugar; mix well. Add eggs, one at a time, beating after each addition. Add sour cream, vanilla and mix well. Pour mixture into pan and bake at 375 degrees for 45 minutes. Do not open the oven door after time is up; turn oven off and leave cake in the oven 1 hour. Cool. Refrigerate in pan for 24 hours.

First Prize Winner, 1980
6 ounces Zwieback cookies
¾ cup sugar
1 teaspoon cinnamon
¼ pound butter

1 ½ pounds cream cheese
4 egg whites
1 cup sugar
1 ½ teaspoons vanilla extract

2 cups sour cream
2 tablespoons sugar
½ teaspoon vanilla extract
⅓ cup almonds, slivered
1 tablespoon butter, for rim

Preheat oven to 375 degrees. Use the steel blade of the food processor; drop the Zwieback cookies into the processor, one at a time, and process until fine. Add the sugar and cinnamon. Melt butter and pour in. Process 2 seconds or until crumbs are moistened. Reserve ¾ cup of crumbs. Press the rest into bottom and sides of a buttered 10-inch springform pan. Bake 10 minutes; refrigerate 30 minutes. Wash the food processor bowl. Preheat oven to 350 degrees. Cut the cheese into one ounce pieces. Process with steel blade until smooth. In another bowl, beat the eggs until stiff. Blend sugar into the egg whites and pour into processor bowl. Process with cream cheese until smooth. Add vanilla. Process for 2 seconds. Pour mixture into crust and bake for 25 minutes. Preheat oven to 475 degrees. Mix together the sour cream, sugar and vanilla. Pour and spread over the top of cake. Sprinkle reserved crumbs to cover topping. Arrange slivered almonds over the crumbs. Bake for 7 minutes. Refrigerate overnight. The next morning, open the springform pan and knock off excess crust.

First Prize Winner, 1968
Beverly Gillia

4 (8-ounce) containers whipped cream cheese
16 ounces sour cream
¼ pound (1 stick) butter
5 eggs
2 tablespoons cornstarch
1¼ cups sugar
1¼ teaspoons vanilla extract
1 teaspoon lemon juice

Let cream cheese, sour cream, butter and eggs stand at room temperature for 1 hour. Blend cream cheese, butter and sour cream together. Add cornstarch, sugar, vanilla and lemon juice. With mixer set on high speed, beat until well blended or you will have lumps of cornstarch. Beat in one egg at a time. Continue beating until mixture is very smooth. Pour mixture into greased 9½-inch springform pan. Place in large roasting pan filled with enough water to come halfway up the side of cake pan. Bake at 375 degrees for 1 hour or until top is golden brown. Turn off oven; let the cake cool in oven for 1 hour.

Remove pan and let it cool for 2 hours on wire rack. Cover the cake and refrigerate for at least 6 hours.

Ricotta Cheesecake
Contestant Entry, late 1970s (courtesy bakeawaywithme.com)

2 8-ounce packages cream cheese, softened
1 15-ounce container ricotta cheese
1½ cups sugar
4 eggs, slightly beaten
2 teaspoons lemon juice
1 teaspoon vanilla extract
3 tablespoons cornstarch
3 tablespoons flour
¼ pound (1 stick) butter, melted and cooled
1 pint sour cream

Preheat oven to 325 degrees. Lightly grease a 9-inch springform pan. Cream together cream cheese and ricotta in a large bowl until combined and creamy. Add the sugar, mixing on medium-low speed until incorporated and smooth. Add the eggs, one at a time, and beat well on medium speed after each addition. Stir in the lemon juice and vanilla. Add the cornstarch and flour; mix in. Add melted butter and mix well. Finally, add the sour cream, stirring well. Pour the mixture into the prepared springform pan.

Bake in a preheated oven for 1 hour. After time is up, turn off the oven and leave cheesecake undisturbed for another 2 hours. When cake is removed from the oven, allow it to cool at room temperature completely before it is refrigerated. Serve chilled.

Mango Cheesecake
First Prize, 1978

CRUST:
6 tablespoons butter, melted and cooled
1 cup graham cracker crumbs
½ cup finely chopped pecans, almonds, or walnuts
2 tablespoons sugar

FILLING:

4 8-ounce packages Philadelphia cream cheese
1 ¼ cups sugar
1 cup sour cream
2 tablespoons cornstarch
¼ teaspoon salt
4 large eggs, room temperature
¼ cup frozen orange juice concentrate
1 teaspoon orange extract
½ teaspoon lemon extract
1 ½ tablespoons grated orange zest

MANGO TOPPING:

½ cup apricot preserves
2 large ripe mangoes to make 1 ½ cups mango slices

Preheat your oven to 350 degrees. Use center rack of oven. Place a sheet pan in the oven to preheat. Prepare 9½- to 10-inch springform pan by taking the bottom and wrapping it in tin foil. This tip is worth the whole show. This way you can easily remove the cake from the bottom, and it also seems to help the pan seal better. Butter or spray foil covering the bottom and sides of the pan.

To make the crust, combine the melted butter with the graham cracker crumbs, the finely chopped nuts and the sugar and press into the bottom and up the sides about 1 ½ inches. Chill until ready to use.

To make filling, use the paddle attachment of your electric mixer and beat the cream cheese until very smooth and soft. Add the sugar and scrape down the bowl to avoid lumps sticking to the side. Beat in the sour cream, cornstarch and salt. Add the eggs one at a time, mixing well between additions. Finally, add in orange juice concentrate, extracts and zest. Scoop batter into prepared pan and place on hot sheet pan already in the oven.

Bake for 35–43 minutes until top is nicely browned. Cake should jiggle but not appear liquid. Cake will firm up as it cools. Cake may form circular cracks around the outside edge, but these will heal as it cools. Set it on a wire rack to cool away from drafts. To prevent further cracks, cover top with a cardboard cake circle and let cool completely at room temperature, then refrigerate. Let cake sit overnight. Run a sharp knife around the edge of the cake and release the springform

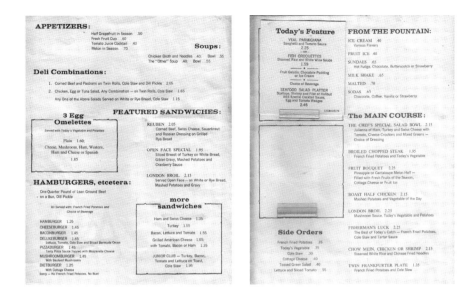

This menu from 1973 was uniformly used throughout all A&S store restaurants.

clip. Now easily pick up the cake, unwrap the tin foil from the bottom and lift the cake onto a platter.

About 1 hour before serving, prepare the mango topping. Put apricot preserves in a small saucepan over low heat to melt it and then strain out the chunks and set aside. Take your beautiful, ripe, thinly sliced mango and arrange them on the top of the cheesecake. Brush it with the apricot glaze, refrigerate for 30 minutes and then serve.

Notes

Chapter 1

1. James L. Ford, "Recollections of Brooklyn in the Sixties," *New York Herald Tribune*, May 31, 1925.
2. *Brooklyn Daily Eagle*, "Joseph Wechsler's Death," October 22, 1896.
3. Ibid., "A Lady's Peril," October 29, 1887.
4. Ibid., "Dissolution of Wechsler & Abraham," December 18, 1892.
5. *Up to the Minute News from Century-Old A&S*, "Moments of Courage: The A&S Moves Toward Greatness," February 16, 1865.
6. *Brooklyn Daily Eagle*, advertisement, October 15, 1867.
7. Walter Rothschild's fortieth-anniversary celebration dinner, private recording, December 1, 1953.
8. *Brooklyn Daily Eagle*, "Observer Tells of Brooklyn's Growth," May 3, 1908.
9. Ibid., "In Their New Building," February 14, 1885.
10. Ibid., "Abraham Abraham's Rise from Employ to Great Merchant," June 28, 1911.

Chapter 2

11. *The First Century of Abraham & Straus: Recording Its 100-Year Love Affair with Its Community*, company brochure, February 14, 1965.
12. *A&S Anniversary Album of Memories*, company brochure, 1945.
13. *Brooklyn Daily Eagle*, "Municipal Matters," February 7, 1884.

14. Ibid., "Wechsler & Abraham Fall Opening," September 23, 1885.
15. Ibid., "Wechsler & Abraham in Their New Building," February 14, 1885.
16. Ibid.
17. Ibid., May 3, 1908.
18. Ibid., "The Firm of Wechsler & Abraham Enlarging Store Facilities," April 28, 1886.
19. *New York Times*, "The Work of a Dastard," October 30, 1887.
20. *Brooklyn Daily Eagle*, "What Crank Wrote This? Some Absurd Talk about an Infernal Machine," December 18, 1888.
21. *First Century of Abraham & Straus*.
22. *Brooklyn Daily Eagle*, "Abraham & Straus, 70 Years Old Today; First Advertisement in the *Eagle*," March 14, 1935.
23. Ibid., "Wechsler & Abraham: The Establishment of the Pioneers in the Uptown Movement," July 27, 1892.
24. Ibid., "Wechsler & Abraham," December 15, 1892.
25. Ibid., "Dissolution of Wechsler & Abraham," December 18, 1892.
26. Ibid., "Urge Wechsler & Abraham," December 24, 1892, 4.

Chapter 3

27. Ibid., editorial, April 1, 1893.
28. *New York Times*, "Rowland H. Macy, Merchant, Obituary," March 31, 1877.
29. *Brooklyn Daily Eagle*, "Joseph Wechsler's Sons," February 14, 1893.
30. Ibid., "Joseph Wechsler's Death," October 22, 1896.
31. Ibid., "To Build a Fine Annex," May 16, 1896.
32. Ibid., "A Big Brooklyn Store: How It Is Conducted," December 11, 1898.
33. City of New York, "The 100th Anniversary of the Consolidation of the Five Boroughs into New York City," http://home.nyc.gov/html/nyc100/html/classroom/hist_info/100boro.html.
34. *First Century of Abraham & Straus*.
35. *Brooklyn Daily Eagle*, May 3, 1908.
36. Ibid., "Abraham & Straus Store Increased in Size," November 4, 1900.

Chapter 4

37. Tom Mahoney and Leonard Sloane, *The Great Merchants* (New York: Harper & Row, 1966), 150.

38. *First Century of Abraham & Straus*, 12.

39. *Brooklyn Daily Eagle*, May 3, 1908.

40. Ibid., "Abraham Abraham, Head of Big Firm, Dies Unexpectedly," June 28, 1911.

41. Ibid., editorial, June 28, 1911.

42. Ibid., "Abraham & Straus Employees Pay Tribute," June 28, 1911.

43. Jan Whitaker, *Service and Style: How the American Department Store Fashioned the Middle Class* (New York: St. Martin's Press, 2006), 63.

44. *Brooklyn Daily Eagle*, "Local Merchants Unite to Make Downtown Brooklyn Greater New York City's Most Attractive Retail Shopping Center," December 22, 1929.

45. Ibid., "Firms Spent $8 Million on Fulton Street," December 22, 1929.

Chapter 5

46. *New York Times*, "Nathan Straus Dies; Nation Mourns Loss of Philanthropist," January 12, 1931.

47. *Brooklyn Daily Eagle*, "Abraham & Straus Subway Store Coming Monday October 8," October 4, 1925.

48. Ibid., "Abraham & Straus to Celebrate 54th Anniversary," February 3, 1924.

49. Ibid., "Abraham & Straus's Sixty Year Public Celebration Opens," February 2, 1925.

50. Ibid., "Boro's Model Home Exhibit Soon Ready; Insured as Museum," September 8, 1925.

51. *New York Times*, "Abraham & Straus Offer Stock Today," December 7, 1925.

52. *Brooklyn Daily Eagle*, "Shop Talk for Man Hunters," May 26, 1947.

53. *New York Times*, "Bloomingdale's Joins Huge Store Merger," September 17, 1929.

54. *Brooklyn Daily Eagle*, "Good Support Halts Selling," July 1, 1929.

55. George E. Berkley and Adolph Caso, *The Filenes* (New York: Branden, 2009), 237.

56. Ibid.

Chapter 6

57. *Brooklyn Daily Eagle*, "Abraham & Straus Head Optimistic," November 19, 1929.
58. *First Century of Abraham & Straus*, 17.
59. Violet Brown, "New Elephant Christened 'Astra' Before 13,000 Children," *Brooklyn Daily Eagle*, October 16, 1938.
60. *Brooklyn Daily Eagle*, "Brooklyn and Forsythia," April 3, 1952.
61. Ibid., "Brooklyn Store Issues Detailed Report for 1940," April 7, 1941.
62. David Robinson, "Black Spider Doomed to Die in Three Days," *Brooklyn Daily Eagle*, May 26, 1940.
63. *Brooklyn Daily Eagle*, "SRO Sign Out on Fulton Street, Brings Down House as Well as Black Spider," June 18, 1940.
64. Ibid., "Abraham & Straus Serves Brooklyn with a New Building," June 24, 1947.

Chapter 7

65. *Brooklyn Daily Eagle*, "Great Stores Made Fulton Street Famous as Shopping Center," October 26, 1941.
66. Isadore Barmash, "Martins, Brooklyn's Oasis of Shopping Calm," *New York Times*, June 16, 1966.
67. Ibid.
68. *Brooklyn Daily Eagle*, "Historic Loeser's Should Not Disappear from Brooklyn," January 27, 1952.
69. Ibid., "Loeser Opens Modern Store in Garden City," May 16, 1937.
70. Ibid., October 26, 1941.
71. Ibid., "Abraham & Straus Takes Over Loeser's Store in Garden City," September 20, 1950.
72. Ibid., "Loeser Sets Liquidation for Thursday," February 10, 1952.
73. *Brooklyn Life and Activities*, "8 Story Addition Is the Tallest Retail Structure in Brooklyn," February 14, 1925.
74. Store advertisement, March 9, 1952.
75. *Brooklyn Daily Eagle*, "Namm-Loeser's Carries on a Tradition," March 9, 1952.
76. New York City Signs, "Oppenheim, Collins & Co.," 2011, https://www.14to42.net/35streetw054.html.

77. Isadore Barmash, *More than They Bargained For: The Rise and Fall of Korvettes* (New York: Lebhar-Friedman/Chain Store Publishing, 1981).
78. *New York Times*, "Brooklyn Losing Specialty Store," September 28, 1956.
79. *Brooklyn Daily Eagle*, "Loeser Building Bought by Mays Store Head," April 11, 1952.
80. Ibid., "Mays Plans Branch at Levittown Center," July 8, 1954.

Chapter 8

81. Federated Department Stores *Annual Report*, 1960, 11.
82. Levitt and Sons Communities, levittownbeyond.com.
83. Federated Department Stores *Annual Report*, 1951.
84. *New York Times*, "W.J. Rothschild, A&S, 68, Dies," October 9, 1960.
85. *Brooklyn Daily Eagle*, "Shop Talk for Man Hunters," December 16, 1946.
86. Federated Department Stores *Annual Report*, 1959.
87. *Womens Wear Daily*, "Macy's, A&S Caught with Their Pants Down," 1961, 116.
88. Byron Porterfield, "Big Garden-Like Mall Dedicated at Huntington," *New York Times*, November 24, 1962.
89. Store advertisement, February 27, 1952.

Chapter 9

90. *New York Herald Tribune*, "Brooklyn Love Affair: 100 Years of Abraham & Straus," February 16, 1965.
91. *A&S Spotlight*, "Go Down to the Farm," March 1965, 12.
92. Isadore Barmash, "Abraham & Straus Going to the North Shore," *New York Times*, May 3, 1965.
93. *A&S Specials*, "Someone Who Remembers," December 1979.
94. Isadore Barmash, "Big in Brooklyn, and in Trouble," *New York Times*, February 10, 1980.
95. Ibid., "Brooklyn's Fulton Street Stores Face Rivals Calmly," *New York Times*, January 5, 1968.
96. Bernadine Morris, "Abraham & Straus and Altman's Mark Centennials by Planning for Future," *New York Times*, April 1, 1965.

Chapter 10

97. Federated Department Stores *Annual Report*, 1970.

98. Isadore Barmash, "Remodeled A&S Tells What's in Store: A New Stress on Fashion," *New York Times*, October 18, 1975.

99. Ibid., "A&S Joins New York Thrust into Jersey," *New York Times*, March 4, 1971.

100. Ibid., "Two Big Retailers Open Branches," *New York Times*, September 13, 1973.

101. Fred Ferretti, "Paramus: A New Mall, Maybe the Last, Rises for Shoppers," *New York Times*, December 10, 1972.

102. Isadore Barmash, "A&S's Bid for Suburban Profit: New Store Aims for Wider Base," *New York Times*, July 25, 1980.

103. *Asbury Park Press*, store advertisement, April 23, 1978.

104. Bob Kappstatter, "Martin's Closing Downtown Store," *New York Daily News*, April 24, 1979.

Chapter 11

105. Mary Martin Niepold, "At Abraham & Straus: A Sneak Preview," *Philadelphia Inquirer*, July 19, 1981.

106. *Store Focus*, 1982, 8.

107. *A&S Spotlight*, "Sunrise—Another Hit in A&S's Long Line of Openings," May 1982.

108. Ibid., "Happy Birthday, Dear Bridge," 1983, 3.

109. Jesus Rangel, "Two Years After Renovation, Brooklyn's Fulton Mall Still Seeks an Anchor," *New York Times*, June 14, 1986.

Chapter 12

110. Isadore Barmash, "B. Altman Conversion Advancing," *New York Times*, May 21, 1985.

111. Gary Cohen and Jennifer Lin, "Strawbridge Will Buy 2 A&S Stores," *Philadelphia Inquirer*, October 30, 1986.

112. Isadore Barmash, "A&S Moves to Fill Gimbels' Void," *New York Times*, March 18, 1989.

113. Rick Fulman, "A&S Plaza, Prospects Are Looking Up for Midtown Mall," *New York Daily News*, February 19, 1989.

114. Carol J. Lormis, "The Biggest Looniest Deal Ever," *Fortune*, June 18, 1990.

115. Christine Dugas, "Does A&S Have a Tomorrow?," *Newsday*, April 11, 1988.

116. Ibid., "A&S Laying Off 794 Employees," *Newsday*, June 7, 1988.

117. Ibid., "A&S Gets All Dolled Up for Its Manhattan Debut," *Newsday*, April 17, 1989.

118. Woody Hochswender, "A&S Makes a Big Bet in Manhattan Retailing," *New York Times*, September 5, 1989.

119. *New York Times*, "Federated to Close Two Stores," September 20, 2000.

120. Edward R. Silverman, "A Landmark in Jeopardy," *Newsday*, March 15, 1990.

121. Suzanne Bilello and Carrie Mason-Draffen, "A&S Makes It Official; Hempstead Landmark to Close Soon," *Newsday*, June 17, 1992.

122. Eben Shapiro, "Two Retailers See End to Chapter 11," *New York Times*, January 11, 1992.

123. Frederic M. Biddle, "Jordan Marsh Says 'Goodbye Boston, Hello Brooklyn,'" *Boston Globe*, April 5, 1992.

124. Telephone conversation with Scott Snyder.

125. Suzanne Bilello, "Sign of Recovery: New Stores Underline Federated's Aggressive Plan for Recovering from Bankruptcy," *Newsday*, October 12, 1992.

126. Patrick M. Reilly and Laura Jereski, "Macy, Federated Reach Accord in Merger Talks," *Wall Street Journal*, July 15, 1994.

127. Stephanie Strom, "Macy Executives Agree to Merger with Federated," *New York Times*, July 14, 1994.

128. Khurran Saeed, "A&S Draws Many Cheers, Crowds, Cars," *Journal News*, November 13, 1994.

129. Diane Alaimo, "After All the Mergers, Stern's Replaces A&S," *Journal News*, April 29, 1995.

130. Ylonda Gault, "A&S cum Stern's: Swap or Stop Gap," *Crain's New York Business*, January 23, 1995.

Chapter 13

131. Terry Pristin, "Remaking the Manhattan Mall: Owner Sees Stern's Departure as Chance to Freshen Up," *New York Times*, September 30, 2000.
132. Christopher Gray, "Different Name, Same Architecture," *New York Times,* July 24, 2005.
133. *Brooklyn Daily Eagle*, "Macy's Reveals Details of Fulton Mall Store Makeover," August 12, 2015.

Index

About the Author

Michael Lisicky is a nationally recognized department store historian, lecturer and author. His books have received critical acclaim in such major newspapers as the *Washington Post*, the *Philadelphia Inquirer*, the *Boston Globe*, the *Newark Star-Ledger*, the *Bergen Record* and the *Baltimore Sun*. His book *Gimbels Has It!* was cited as "one of the freshest reads of 2011" by National Public Radio's *Morning Edition* program. Mr. Lisicky has given lectures at such locations as the New York Public Library, the Boston Public Library, New York Fashion Week and the D.C. Public Library, as well as at the 2011 Wanamaker Organ Centennial Week celebration in Philadelphia. He also served as a historical consultant for the Oscar-nominated film *Carol* and has been featured in the *New York Times*, *Wall Street Journal* and on National Public Radio and CBS's *Sunday Morning* television program. Mr. Lisicky resides in Baltimore, where he is also an oboist with the Baltimore Symphony Orchestra. He is also the author of *Baltimore Symphony Orchestra: A Century of Sound*.